MW00532953

DOMINICAN
SPIRITUALITY

Principles and Practice

By
WILLIAM A. HINNEBUSCH, O.P.

Illustrations by
SISTER MARY OF THE COMPASSION, O.P.

WIPF & STOCK · Eugene, Oregon

Nihil obstat:

Rev. Paul K. Meagher, O.P.

Censor Deputatus

Imprimatur:

✠ Patrick A. O'Boyle

Archbishop of Washington

December 10, 1964

Wipf and Stock Publishers
199 W 8th Ave, Suite 3
Eugene, OR 97401

Dominican Spirituality
Principles and Practice
By Hinnebusch, William A., O.P.
Copyright©1965 Domincan House of Studies - The Thomist
ISBN 13: 978-1-62564-470-1
Publication date 11/1/2014
Previously published by Dominican Publications, 1965

To the Lady of the Rosary

AT AN INN, ON THE WAY

For ten years my community of Friars entrusted me with the responsibility and privilege of the *traditio*: of handing on our Dominican way of life to Novices. There was never really any way to tell them about it before they were living it. Before they ever cracked the Book of Constitutions, they were wearing the habit, serving as cantors at Office, and being introduced to parishioners as "Brother." In the end, it was the living of the life that transmitted its spirit, and the active ingredient in the living was conversation. Of course we occupied the forums of dialogue specified by our tradition; the classroom, the chapter room, and the common room. But the glue came in the un-planned interchanges while washing dishes, shoveling snow, or picking the hymns for the week. We became brothers through the exchanges so ordinary that we do not remember them.

People who talk about the Dominican Order, from what-ever angle, end up telling you about its whole way of life. Fr. Hinnebusch is no exception. To treat of our spirituality, he cannot focus on a pattern of interior prayer, common devo-tion, ministerial endeavor, or even the spiritual place of study in its life. He has to look at everything we do and the history of it. Here we get what makes his work comprehensive as a presentation and insightful for our age. The distinctiveness of any Dominican thing-- prayer, intellectual life, government, asceticism, and even preaching--consists in its relationship to the other things. Fr. Hinnebusch offers us an expanded for

I

publication version of the talk we all give when asked about our way of life.

An incident in St. Dominic's life distills the power of Dominican life into a moment. Once, during a preaching journey, he sat up all night with a heretical innkeeper, and talked with him until he returned to the faith. Presumably Dominic did something more than wear down his interlocutor: he engaged the proprietor in that comprehensive encounter we call a conversation. In a virtual age, we must specify that a conversation demands more than an exchange of words.It requires a bodily encounter, in which tone of voice, eye movement, and posture complement and nuance words. In such a moment, I may utter words you disagree with utterly, but you will listen to them if I establish as a context my absolute respect for your person and your sincerity. The supple listening and speaking of a true conversation establish a place of safety and engagement that in turn fosters communion.

The vignette comes down to us a something more than a tribute to St. Dominc's undoubted charisma and social skill. He came to that moment as a preacher in the mode he wished to establish for his order. He gave the man orthodoxy in words shaped for him. Molding the preaching were the years of intense living with others, as a student, a cathedral canon, and with his brothers. It got its edge from study: Dominic was conversant with his own tradition, but also came to understand the teaching and aspirations of the heretics. Sustaining him in these challenging encounters was the love he had for their souls, acquired in, and sustained by, liturgical and private prayer. Also, we do not catch the power of this meeting without reference to the Evangelical Counsels. These habits of life made Dominic, the obedient man, available to the work of the Holy Spirit in this moment. Likewise the poor man was undefended, and the chaste man without manipulation. Paradox provided a final readiness, for Dominic came to this moment equipped by a monastic life to be outside of his monastery, a man so apart from that he could be radically present to.

Dominic's presence to the conversation with the innkeeper flowed from the conversation among the elements of his life. The integral working of these flies off Fr. Hinnebusch's pages. Study flows from a contemplative foundation and nourishes contemplative prayer. The observances of community life give shape to ministry and are in turn enriched by it. Liturgical prayer shares a linguistic common ground with intellectual endeavor. Even the Order's pattern of governance demands conversation at local, regional, and universal levels. Its legislation takes shape from a fraternal argument and development of consensus. Even St. Dominic obeyed the conversation of his brothers when it countered his own preference.

Perhaps one could say that the spirituality of a Dominican lies in the willingness to engage in lifelong conversation: with God in the liturgy, with the tradition in study, with the brothers in chapter, and God's people in ministry. To choose such a path is to accept a way that demands vulnerability, patience, and humility. At the same time, this way of the dialogue gives a constant reassurance that one is in touch with reality.

Conversation unbound describes the stability and dynamism of Dominican life, and indeed its present happiness. When that life is fully lived, it features continuous interchange, unfolding in a variety of forums at the same time. Dominic placed his followers well within the monastic, dialogical tradition of the Divine Office, in which the speaking and hearing of the psalmody and canticles so interpenetrate as to immerse the mind and senses in and encounter with the Living Word. That this makes for spirits that are at the same time assertive and receptive appears in the *Dialogues* of St. Catherine of Siena. She stands before us as a woman in conversation with her God, but also with her Church, and her contemporaries, all of which is of a piece with her prayer.

Dominican intellectual life consists less in mastering or mining a text than it does in having a good back and forth with a friend, whom one has already met, and knows will meet again. Thus the Sacred Scriptures take pride of place in our study for they form the textual centerpiece of our life. The reassurance they offer provides the safety in which to struggle with the perplexities they generate. Consider that the greatest intellectual ornament of the Order, the *Summa Theologiae* of St. Thomas Aquinas, takes the form of a dialogue. The Angelic Doctor presents his teachings as the fruit of conversations with the Scriptures, with the Fathers, and with his colleagues, many of whom were fellow Dominicans. Thomas also converses with Aristotle: he both learns from him and goes beyond him. In speaking with him, Thomas speaks with the ferment of his own time, in reverence and in critique. The Order has always understood that Thomas sustained intellectual vulnerability, and achieved intellectual credibility, on a foundation of contemplative religious observance, and with a longing for God Himself. Thus the *Summa* possesses the same energy as Dominic's late night session in the taproom.

Dominicans of all kinds participate in their own governance through the dialogue of chapter. At local, regional, and global levels, we examine our life and mission, and recommit to both. In the chapter room, the Holy Spirit presides in such a way that the true issues of the group are evaded only by conspiracy. The virtues of chapter are candor, courage, and humility, and the conversation must be safe enough, and demanding enough, to draw them out. Here the shape of St. Dominic's charity toward the innkeeper may be ours as we determine to go the distance with one another in the pursuit of God. In chapter each part of the Order also communicates with the other parts. We elect delegates to go higher chapters, so that they can be listened to by delegates from other localities. We legislate for lower chapters to receive, talk about, and implement in their circumstances.

A whole catalog of reasons why the spirituality of the preachers treasures the face to face! One must concede the cumbersome and inefficient patterns this approach enshrines. What it yields is a truly human pattern of prayer and life that speaks to the pain and the longings of the age. In a world where words are typed out furiously and shot off into cyberspace, we have much to learn from a tradition which presumes that we do not utter a syllable without having wrestled with it first ourselves. While our contemporaries browse through an information explosion, Dominicans sustain long conversations with familiar texts in study and in prayer. Going the distance with ideas and texts does not happen without persevering with people.

The joy and asceticism of common life ultimately safeguard the suppleness and discipline demanded by the Dominican contemplative and intellectual life. From these crucibles we derive the capacity to distinguish movements of the Spirit from the ideologies that march across the stage of the moment. In prayer with God, and in comprehensive interchange with a Dominican community, we can stay connected to the real. In a spirituality of conversation lies a way to a proper sense of proportion, and to emotional stability. With these we can give pastoral help to a culture addicted to crisis. If we follow our heritage of critical conversation with the Age, we can offer it the perspective of God's presence discernible in history.

Fr. Hinnebusch conceived the talks that gave rise to this work in 1962, as the Church was poised on the cusp of the Second Vatican Council. While the Council is long concluded, the conversation begun there has not. As I write these words we have begun the pontificate of Pope Francis and the work of the last five decades will undergo a new review. We are in conversation with what has been written and what has been done. For all of this time we have been reacting to Vatican II. It will be exemplary of Dominican spirituality to return to the texts of the Council and reread them in the creative tension of what is static, and what is in movement. Such is the dialogue of the tradition of the Order with those who inhabit it at any age. The willingness to reread is the willingness to stay in conversation, and to stay in movement toward God. It is the conversation that establishes the safety that makes us able to keep setting out.

When we preach we are at an inn on the way, and our conversation draws on the journey we have taken, and on the home we have not yet reached.

Walter Wagner, O.P.
St Vincent Ferrer Priory
New York City
March 2014

FOREWORD

Most of this book originated in a series of conferences to the Dominican Sisters of the Congregation of the Most Holy Cross, Amityville, New York, at Dominican Commercial High School, Jamaica, L. I., during the Lent of 1962. All the conferences have been rewritten with some minor deletions and the addition of considerable new material. The first chapter is added as a general introduction to Dominican life to serve as a unifying principle for the rest of the book.

I have also adapted the material to the needs of a wider reading audience. No longer do I address the sister but the Dominican. While some matter applies specifically to nuns or sisters, the use of masculine nouns and pronouns elsewhere by no means indicates that I am addressing only the members of the First Order. Though the forms and methods of their spiritual life vary to some degree (especially that of the secular tertiary), all Dominicans share the same basic vocation and follow the same spiritual path.

I must thank the sisters of the Amityville community for their interest in the conferences, the sisters of Dominican Commercial High School for taping and mimeographing them, the fathers and the sisters of other Congregations who suggested that a larger audience might welcome them. I am grateful to the fathers especially of the Dominican House of Studies, Washington, D. C., who counselled me, discussed doctrinal points with me, and, by their urging encouraged me to make the revision and prepare the material for publication. A word of thanks is owed to Sister Mary of the Compassion, O.P., of Our Lady of the Rosary Monastery, Union City, N. J., for permission to use her illustrations of St. Dominic. My friend, Miss Elsie Fillo, an apostolic tertiary, has been most faithful and competent in typing the manuscript. The following publishers have kindly permitted me to quote from their books: P. J. Kenedy and Sons from Raymond of Capua's *Life of St. Catherine of Siena*, The Priory Press from Henry Suso's *Exemplar*, and Helicon Press from Foster's *Life of Saint Thomas Aquinas, Biographical Documents.* The translation of the lyric of Sister Sourire's *Dominique* is used with permission.

W.A.H.

May 1, 1965

Washington, D. C.

TABLE OF CONTENTS

Illustrations by Sister Mary of the Compassion, O.P.

INTRODUCTION

In this day when men and women are earnestly searching for authenticity and relevance in their own lives as well as in the Church in order to be more effective witnesses of Christ in the world, we as Dominicans must also seriously investigate our own origins, so that we too might use all our talents to serve the Church. For this is the purpose of our existence, to worship God according to a particular mode of life approved by the Church and thereby realize our own personal sanctification and the specific end for which we were founded.

It is only by a constant renewal of ourselves that we can even hope to realize the ideal given to us by our holy Father St. Dominic. Renewal is not just a matter of new external forms of activity but should rather affect one's interior disposition and attitude. We must adapt ourselves to change and at the same time enter more deeply into the spirit of St. Dominic. The pages that follow give us a penetrating view of Dominican life. I think this book will be warmly received because of the great lack of such spiritual works in English. Furthermore, it makes its appearence at an appropriate time when the religious life is being severely criticized and its validity in the modern world being challenged.

In reading any book about Dominican spirituality, there is always a danger of our unconsciously seeking refuge and comfort in a romanticized past rather than facing up to the problems of the contemporary situation in which we find ourselves. The dichotomy creates tension when there is little or no relationship between the real and the ideal order of things. We must constantly work to bridge the gap so that we will be imitating St. Dominic in spirit and in truth. There is really no need for Dominicans to protest their loyalty to our heritage.

Good will is presumed but it is necessary for us to take a step further; to live the Dominican ideal to the best of our ability in whatever apostolic activity we have been assigned to perform. In the concrete, this is the only way in which we can realize our usefulness in Christ and make a positive contribution to the continued growth of the Church. May we, with the help of God's grace, strive to measure up to the ideal and reflect an authentic image of St. Dominic in our lives.

R. L. EVERY, O.P.
Provincial
St. Joseph Province

April 20, 1965

Chapter I

A GENERAL VIEW
of
DOMINICAN LIFE

The Dominican enters the Order of Friars Preachers to save his soul. He could have saved it outside the Order, but, once he takes vows, must save it through the spirituality of the Order. Nothing could be more vital for him, therefore, than to understand Dominican spirituality. It is composed of the end St. Dominic chose for his Order and the means he established to realize this end. In practice, the Order's spirituality means living the religious life as it is prescribed in the Rule of St. Augustine, the Constitutions, and the family customs which have developed over the centuries. If the Dominican lives these things established for him, he follows a spirituality that will lead him to salvation.

St. Dominic embraced the same general elements of the Christian life shared by others in the Church, but blended them into a specific spirituality that is original, balanced, and unique. The spiritual life of the Friars Preachers draws from Sacred Scripture, bases itself on the Holy Sacrifice of the Mass, the Sacraments, and the liturgy, incorporates principles of traditional asceticism, and drinks from the purest sources of Western mysticism and monasticism. It shares characteristics found in the spirituality of the clergy, in earlier monasticism, and in

1

the evangelical movements of the twelfth and thirteenth centuries. But the Order of Preachers has given all these common elements a Dominican emphasis. Even where its spirituality most closely touches that of another group, such as the Franciscans, it emphasizes shared elements in a distinctive way. For example, though poverty is a major characteristic of the spiritual life of Dominicans, it has never dominated the spiritual horizon as it does among Franciscans. Instead Dominican life has pivoted around the preaching apostolate.

The spirituality of the Friars Preachers is exceedingly lofty. It is theocentric, Christological, sacerdotal (in origin, the Order is a branch of Canons Regular and is, therefore, predominantly priestly in membership), monastic, contemplative, and apostolic. It is, in truth, the spirituality of Christ the Preacher and of the Apostles. The primary intention is to elevate the friar to the heights of contemplation, but going beyond this, Dominican contemplation itself is intended to fructify in the apostolate for souls, especially through preaching, teaching, and writing. Contemplation is the generic element, the one the Friars Preachers share with other contemplative Orders; the salvation of souls through preaching is the specific note distinguishing Dominicans from all other Orders. The Constitutions clearly indicate this twofold character:

> The principal reason we are gathered together is that we dwell together in harmony and have one mind and one heart in God, in other words, that we be found perfect in charity . . . Our Order is known to have been founded from the beginning expressly for preaching and the salvation of souls. . . . This end we ought to pursue, preaching and teaching from the abundance and fulness of contemplation in imitation of our most holy Father Dominic, who spoke only with God or of God for the benefit of souls.

The Second Order places the same double purpose before its members: "The nuns of the sacred Order of

Preachers . . . strive after Christian perfection; and by means of that perfection, implore for the labors of their brethren abundant fruit in holiness." The same orientation of spirituality is found in the Constitutions of the sisters of the Third Order:

> The principal and essential end of our Congregation is the personal sanctification of the sisters. The secondary or special end is the education of Catholic youth, care of orphans, the nursing of the sick, or the conducting of retreat houses.

Members of the secular Third Order, tertiaries, endeavor to sanctify themselves according to the Dominican spirit. Their Rule adapts the basic ends of the Order to their life as members of the laity:

> The end of the Third Order is the sanctification of its own members by the practice of a more perfect Christian life and the promotion of the salvation of souls in a way that is suitable to the state of the faithful living in the world.

The contemplative aspect of the Order's life is found especially in elements borrowed fom the monks and canons (see *Summa Theol.*, II—II, q. 188, a. 8, ad 2). The Constitutions enumerate three contemplative features of traditional monasticism among the four fundamental means of attaining the Order's ends, namely, ". . . the three solemn vows of obedience, chastity and poverty, the regular life with its monastic observances, the solemn chanting of the Divine Office, and the assiduous study of sacred truth." These are essential means which can never be radically altered. They separate the Dominican from the world, direct him to God, and oblige him to live a contemplative and penitential life in the pursuit of Christian perfection.

The Contemplative Quality of Dominican Life

The solemn chanting of the Divine Office, especially, disposes the friar for contemplation. It centers his life around the liturgy and nourishes the life of his spirit. In the early Order, two periods of "secret prayers", the one after lauds, the second after compline, prolonged the effect of the canonical hours. In the modern Order, fixed periods of mental prayer continue this early practice. During these "secret prayers," the friars, in imitation of the prayer of St. Dominic, were permitted much liberty of spirit. Some recited vocal prayers, psalms, and *Aves;* others visited altars, making abundant use of gestures, genuflections, and prostrations. St. Dominic himself was always in prayer. The short work, *The Nine Ways of Prayer of St. Dominic,* indicate that he employed a variety of methods and bodily postures. Here is how he occupied himself during the period of secret prayers:

> He had yet another manner of praying at once beautiful, devout, and pleasing, which he practiced after the canonical hours and the thanksgiving following meals. He was then zealous and filled with the spirit of devotion which he drew from the divine words which had been sung in choir or refectory. Our father quickly withdrew to some solitary place, to his cell or elsewhere, and recollected himself in the presence of God. He would sit quietly, and after the sign of the cross, begin to read from a book opened before him. His spirit would then be sweetly aroused as if he heard Our Lord speaking. . . .

St. Dominic taught his friars to contemplate even while on the highways. He would say to his companion: "Let us think of the Savior." He himself often sang the *Veni Creator* or the *Ave Maris Stella* as he walked.

> He delighted in giving himself completely to meditation disposing for contemplation, and he would say to his companion on the journey: "It is written in Osee: 'I will lead her (my spouse) into the wilderness and I will speak to her heart.'" Parting from his companion, he would go on ahead or, more frequently, follow at some distance. Thus withdrawn, he would walk and pray; in his meditation he was inflamed and the fire of charity was enkindled.

He constantly urged his friars "to speak only with God or of God" and had this exhortation incorporated into the Constitutions. For more than seven hundred years, this paternal admonition has stood at the head of the Constitutions. Concerning the special end of the Order, preaching for the salvation of souls, the Constitutions state: "This end we ought to pursue, preaching and teaching from the abundance and fulness of contemplation, in imitation of our holy father Dominic who did not speak except with God or of God for the good of souls." They also admonish the master of novices to instruct his charges about the contemplative end of the Order.

> Before everything else let the novice master teach the novices and earnestly recommend to them that they carry out fully the precept concerning the love of God and neighbor, at the head of the Rule . . . along with the nature and general end of the religious life—the personal sanctification of each member—let the novices be taught the special end of our Order, namely, to communicate to others the things they contemplate in prayer and study. . . .

Dominican spirituality is also penitential. This quality is found especially in the vows, in the regular observances of monasticism, and in the community life. These elements of the Order's life are indeed directed to more sublime purposes than penance, and we shall note these in later chapters, but the friar would be mistaken if he overlooked the many opportunities for mortification and sacrifice that life in the priory presents. We can readily appreciate the penitenial nature of fasting and abstinence, disciplines, silence, the continual attempt to purify conscience according to a comprehensive code of faults to be declared in chapter, and wearing the religious habit. Even the Office chanted together in choir, while serving the supreme ends of religion and promoting the highest spiritual good of the friars, has its penitential aspect. Humbert of Romans refers to this feature of choral recitation: "The greater part of our penance consists in the recitation of the Divine Office."

The penitential character of the Order's regular observances is better appreciated when their source is considered. They were borrowed bodily from the Premonstratentians, who, in turn, took them from the austere Cistercians. The founder accentuated these traditional observances by adding a chapter on silence to the Constitutions and by embracing the severe deprivations of mendicant poverty—a poverty which abandoned fixed revenues and secure income, not only for the individual but for the entire Order. Such total surrender of property entailed a profound reliance on Divine Providence. When the conditions of European life changed, Pope Sixtus IV mitigated this strict regime, in 1475, permitting and commanding all Mendicant Orders, except the Franciscans, to own corporate property. The Order, nevertheless, still looks on poverty as a primary means of asceticism for its members and as an effective instrument of its apostolic work. The poverty of Dominican religious and the moderate character of their houses and convents witness to the "other-worldly" character of the Christian message.

St. Dominic had such a high estimate of the monastic part of the Order's life that he carried it as much as possible into the apostolate.

> Almost always when he was outside the priory, on hearing the first stroke of the matins bell from the monasteries, he used to arise and arouse the friars. With great devotion he celebrated the whole night and day Offices at the prescribed hours so that he omitted nothing. After compline, when traveling, he kept, and had his companions keep, silence, just as though they were in the priory. Then in the morning, while en route, he had them remain silent almost until terce every day. . . . When Brother Dominic was in a priory where he had to make a stop, he conformed to the community in food and drink, kept the rule entirely and fully, and did all he could to have his friars keep it.

Besides their penitential aspects, Dominican community life and observances serve another purpose, forming the friar and preparing him for contemplation. Constant fidelity to the rule imposes considerable self-control on the religious, demands constant scrutiny of conscience and whole-hearted obedience to rule and authority. This regime leads to a more perfect exercise of many virtues. Thus it restrains the natural impetuosity of his senses and emotions, establishes peace in his soul, and nourishes his fraternal charity, a prime requisite for contemplation and apostolic activity.

The Priestly Character of Dominican Life

Since the Order of Friars Preachers is at root, by papal confirmation and the use of the Rule of St. Augustine, an Order of Canons Regular, its spirituality is priestly, theocentric, and Christological. The solemn worship of the Church is a fundamental element in the life of a Canon. By origin, the Canons were officially designated by the Church to continue without interruption the official prayer-life, carrying out in the cathedrals and collegiate churches of the world the solemn acts of the liturgy —the solemn Mass and the solemn chanting of the Divine Office. In framing the Order's first Constitutions, St. Dominic began them with a detailed regulation of the conventual Mass and the singing of matins and the canonical hours. The present Constitutions impose the choral recitation of the Divine Office as an essential means for achieving the aims of Dominican spirituality and the apostolate.

During Dominic's own lifetime, the Order endeavored to establish a uniform rite, so that its children everywhere might praise God through the use of a single liturgy. These efforts did not cease until 1256 when a highly satisfactory Dominican Rite had been developed. Its excellence was so appreciated that many dioceses and other Orders adopted it.

The priestly spirituality of the Friars Preachers has

always accented loyalty to the Church, to the Pope, and
to the truths of the Catholic Faith. From these loyalties
has sprung the Order's marked emphasis on preaching and
the salvation of souls. Primarily, the Order seeks to do
the work of the apostle, propagating the Faith, defending
it, and carrying out the final command of Christ: "Go,
therefore, and make disciples of all nations . . . teaching
them to observe all that I have commanded you" (Matt.
28:19-20).

The love of Catholic truth directed Dominican attention immediately on God, the beginning and end of
all creation, on Christ Jesus, "the way, the truth, and the
life", man's way of return to God, on the Mass and Sacraments (especially the Eucharist), and on Mary, the
Mother of God.

Devotion to Christ

The Order's tender affection for the Person of Christ
arose from the example of St. Dominic, from the pursuit
of personal sanctification by the friars, and from its mission to preach Christ Crucified. Though springing from
these sources, it flowed in channels common to the Middle
Ages. The friars were drawn like their contemporaries
toward the Sacred Humanity of Christ. They manifested
and helped develop the devotions which focused on the
Sacred Passion, the Precious Blood, the Five Wounds, the
Pierced Heart, and the Blessed Sacrament.

> Engrossed in his contemplation of the sufferings
> of Christ, St. Dominic would remain before the
> altar or in the chapter room with his gaze fixed
> on the Crucified One, looking upon Him with per-
> fect attention. He genuflected frequently, again
> and again. He would continue sometimes from
> after compline until midnight, now rising, now
> kneeling, . . . Thus there was formed in our holy
> father, St. Dominic, a great confidence in God's
> mercy. . . .

St. Thomas, earnestly gazing at the crucifix, was raised
upward toward his Crucified Savior and heard him say

from the Cross: "You have written well of me, Thomas. What do you desire as a reward for your labors?" Thomas replied: "Lord, only yourself." Bl. Henry Suso, seeking union with the Divinity, complained to his beloved Eternal Wisdom: "I look everywhere for your divinity but you show me your humanity; I desire your sweetness but you offer me your bitterness; I want to suckle but you teach me to fight." Eternal Wisdom replied:

> No one can arrive at divine heights or taste mystical sweetness without passing through my human bitterness. The higher anyone climbs without passing through my humanity, the deeper will be his fall. Anyone who wishes to attain what you are seeking must tread the road of my humanity and pass through the gate of sufferings. Therefore, dismiss your faintheartedness and join me in the arena of knightly valor. . . .

Henry pioneered in developing the Way of the Cross. He customarily made a hundred meditations on the Passion of Christ which carried him from the Last Supper to Calvary. He began meditating in the chapter room of the priory and progressed, station by station, through cloister into choir, here he ended his devotion at the foot of the crucifix which stood above the screen between nave and choir. During this sorrowful journey he pictured the Passion in detail,

> so that Christ's every pain, from beginning to end, was individually recalled. . . . . . Not content, however, with keeping this devotion to himself, he wanted to share it with other souls who might experience the same difficulty and dryness while meditating on the passion, sole source of our salvation. Therefore, he wrote out the meditations.

Bl. Alvarez of Cordova, returning from a visit to the Holy Land in 1402, conceived the idea of spiritually renewing his pilgrimage by means of tableaux. In the gardens of Scala Coeli, founded by him in 1423, he set up a series of oratories with pictures recalling the holy places in Palestine.

St. Catherine de Ricci, who for twelve years, from 1542 to 1554, experienced an ecstatic vision of the Passion every week, developed a devotion called the *Canticle of the Passion*. Its verses, selected from the Scriptures, are arranged as a summary of Christ's sufferings. The brief meditation made on each verse powerfully impresses the greatness of the Passion on the soul and brings it the fruits of redemption. This devotion is still practiced in some of the priories of the Order. At Santa Sabina, its headquarters in Rome, the Canticle occupies the period of mental prayer on the Fridays of Lent. The cantor, kneeling before the altar, begins the verses, which are taken up by the choir, or he sings them alone. Between each he pauses for some minutes to permit the friars to ponder the verse just sung. As a fitting close to the exercise, though not part of it, he blesses the community with a relic of the True Cross which, meanwhile, has been exposed on the altar, flanked by lighted candles.

Devotion to the suffering Christ focused the attention of the early friars on the Five Wounds. The devotion carried them inward to the Pierced Heart of Christ. Albert the Great saw the Blessed Sacrament as the love-gift of the Divine Heart. Meister Eckhart took a step further; speaking of the Eucharistic Heart, he said:

> We see how heat draws all things to itself . . . with such fire did our Lord Jesus Christ burn on the Cross. His heart burns like a fire and a furnace from which the flames burst forth on all sides. He was thus inflamed on the Cross by his fire of love for the whole world. Therefore, he drew all the world to himself with his heat of love.

Saints Catherine of Siena and Catherine de Ricci experienced an "exchange of hearts" with Christ. In ecstacy, St. Rose of Lima heard him saying, "Rose of my heart, be thou my spouse." St. Martin of Porres merited to drink from the side of Christ.

The wound in the side of Christ, the Precious Blood,

and the Pierced Heart were a constant preoccupation of St. Catherine of Siena. In a beautiful passage in one of her letters, she summarizes the inner meaning of these devotions:

> Place your lips to the side of the Son of God, for it is an opening which emits the fires of charity and pours forth its Blood to wash us from our iniquities. The soul which reposes there and looks with the eyes of its soul on the Heart opened and consumed by love will be made conformable to him, for seeing itself so much loved it cannot fail to love in return. That soul becomes perfect because what it loves it loves for God and it loves nothing outside of him. In desire it becomes to him another self, since it has no other will but that of God.

St. Catherine of Siena, St. Catherine de Ricci, Bl. Lucy of Narni, and, it is estimated, eighty-three other Dominicans were favored with the stigmata.

The Order's devotion to the Holy Name sprang from its preaching mission. By vocation, the Order was commissioned to carry knowledge of this name to every tribe and nation on earth. Henry of Cologne, drawn to the Order in 1220 by Reginald of Orleans, was the first Dominican to manifest this devotion. Jordan of Saxony, who loved Henry as a brother, closes his affectionate summary of his friend's life with these words:

> He was accustomed to propose the Name of Jesus, most worthy of of all reverence and worship, that Name, I say, which is above all names; so much so, that even today when in church or during a sermon this Name is pronounced, the affection of many hearts is immediately stirred to a manifestation of reverence.

Perhaps it was the knowledge of Dominican preaching of this devotion that prompted Pope Gregory X to turn to Bl. John of Vercelli, Master General, for implementation of the decision of the Second Council of Lyons. The Council had decreed that the faithful should be taught to bow their heads when the Holy Name was mentioned in reparation for the blasphemies and irreverence of Christians. Vercelli organized an Order-wide preaching campaign to obey the pope's command. Devotion to the Holy Name was continued in the fourteenth century by the Dominican nuns of the Rhineland under the urging of Blessed Henry Suso, who preached "the love of the sweet name of Jesus far and wide," seeking "with great enthusiasm to enkindle the name of Jesus in all cold hearts."

In the fifteenth century, Dominicans established the Holy Name Society in many places. The most glorious pages in its history, however, were written in the United States by Father Charles Hyacinth McKenna, the "Apostle of the Holy Name and of the Holy Rosary". After Fr. McKenna obtained a papal indult in 1896 permitting its establishment in every church, his preaching made the Society popular throughout the country. The Society has fostered the faith of Catholic men and ensured their frequent reception of the Sacraments. Great Holy Name parades and conventions have given the people of the United States striking manifestation of the Catholic Faith.

A prominent characteristic of the spiritual life of Saints Dominic, Thomas Aquinas, Catherine of Siena, Vincent Ferrer, and many other Dominicans was devotion to the Holy Sacrifice of the Mass and the Blessed Sacrament. Nowhere did St. Thomas display his faith in the Eucharist more forcefully than in his protestation when receiving Holy Viaticum:

> I am receiving thee, O price of my soul's redemption: all my studies, my vigils, and my labors have been for love of thee. I have taught much and written much of the most sacred Body of Jesus Christ; I have taught and written in the faith of Jesus Christ and the holy Roman Church, to whose judgment I offer and submit everything.

The outstanding love of St. Thomas for the Blessed Sacrament, and his writings on the Eucharist merited for him the title "Eucharistic Doctor."

Devotion to Mary

Devotion to the Blessed Virgin, the Mother of God, flowed from Dominican devotion to Christ. The friars were convinced that the Order owed its foundation to her intercession. They placed her name in the profession formula, promising obedience "to God, and the Blessed Mary, and St. Dominic, and the master general." The Order obliged its children to recite Mary's Little Office daily, except on major feasts. The friars celebrated her Saturday Office, her many feasts, solemnly chanted the *Salve Regina* to terminate Compline, visited her altars, saluted her images, and recited the *Ave Maria* hundreds of times daily. Through the Rosary Confraternity, they gave the most excellent Marian devotion to the Church. Focusing attention on the principal mysteries of Our Lord's life, the Rosary, in a sense, epitomizes Dominican spirituality. It summarizes the liturgical cycles, combines tender devotion to Christ and his Mother with strict theology, and leads to contemplation. The Rosary is a way of proclaiming the truths of faith expressed in the form of praise.

Dominican Apostolic Spirituality

St. Dominic joined the spiritual practices of the Order's life and its apostolic activity in an inseparable union. Going beyond traditional monasticism, he made Dominican spirituality apostolic. His own prayer and penance were strongly oriented toward, and motivated by, the salvation of souls. The canonization witnesses unanimously speak of his compassion, prayer, and penance for sinners. His estimate of the apostolic value of penance is well illustrated by an episode that occurred while he was still preaching to the Albigenses. On one occasion, when on their way to debate with heretics, St. Dominic and his companions, including the bishop of the place, walked barefooted at the Saint's suggestion. Losing their way, they asked directions from a native, an Albigensian, who maliciously led them through a thicket where their legs and feet were severly torn by thorns. Then Dominic en-

couraged his companions: "Let us hope in the Lord, for
the victory shall be ours; already our sins are washed
away in blood." Often he took off his shoes when traveling to endure the penance of the stony roads. He was
constantly alert to benefit spiritually by unexpected mortifications. When he stubbed his toes against the stones,
was poorly served at meals, was scoffed at and mistreated
by the Albigenses, his only answer was, "It is a penance."

Dominic's apostolic spirit gained the highest recogni-
tion a few years after his death when his friend, Pope
Gregory IX, prepared to canonize him. When the friars
came to beg this favor from the Pope, he chided them for
being so slow to promote Dominic's cause. "In him," he
said, "I knew a man who lived the rule of the apostles in
its totality." John of Spain during the Canonization process testified:

> He was filled with compassion for his neighbors
> and most ardently desired their salvation. He him-
> self constantly and frequently preached and, in
> every way he could, urged the friars to preach,
> begging and advising them to be solicitous for the
> salvation of souls, and sending them to preach.

Jordan of Saxony wrote of Dominic:

> God gave him the singular grace of weeping for
> sinners, the unfortunate, and the afflicted. He
> carried their miseries in the sanctuary of his com-
> passionate heart and poured forth his burning
> love in floods of tears. Spendng the whole night
> in prayer, he was accustomed to pray to his Father
> over and over again in secret. His frequent and
> special prayer to God was for the gift of true
> charity capable of laboring for and winning the
> salvation of men, since he deemed that he would
> be a true member of Christ only when he could
> devote himself entirely to gaining souls, like the
> Lord Jesus, the Savior of all, who offered himself
> completely for our salvation.

The modern Order cherishes these lessons of St. Dominic. The 1962 general chapter pointed out anew the close

connection between prayer, penance, and the apostolate:

> We earnestly urge and advise our brethren who
> are engaged in the sacred ministry that they make
> the note of austerity which is proper to our Order
> evident also in their apostolate, especially in their
> way of life, clothing, means of transportation, etc.,
> so that their preaching may become more effica-
> cious through the testimony of their lives.

The contemplative Dominican preacher must pursue
evangelical perfection; his must be the spirituality of the
Apostles; he must imitate the Poor Christ of the Gospel,
the Preacher, who, having formed his Apostles, sent them
two by two to preach the Gospel. St. Dominic established
apostolic spirituality as the criterion for his children. They
must imitate the lives of the Apostles and follow the evangelical way of preaching. Here are the instructions for
preachers St. Dominic incorporated into the Constitutions:

> When those who are approved are sent out to
> preach, they shall be assigned companions by the
> prior according as he judges expedient in the light
> of their character and dignity. Receiving a bless-
> ing, they shall then go forth as men desirous of
> their own salvation and the salvation of others.
> Let them act with religious decorum as men of
> the Gospel, following in the footsteps of their Sav-
> ior speaking with God or about God to themselves
> and their neighbors, and being careful to avoid un-
> due familiarity with others. Furthermore, those
> going out to exercise the office of preaching or
> traveling for any other reason shall neither receive
> nor carry with them any gold, silver, money or
> gifts, but only food, clothing, books, and other ne-
> cessities. . . .

The Friars Preachers must strive to be apostles who con-
verse with God or who in the classic phrase of St. Thomas:
"contemplate and give to others the fruit of their contemplation." The rule and Constitutions, and the religious life they establish, are directed to the grand purpose of sanctifying the preacher and making him an apos-

tle. The entire complexus of life in the cloister is designed
to awaken fraternal charity and to lead to contemplation.
These qualities are nourished on the truths of revelation
and sustained by the virtues which are generated and
strengthened by the penitential observances of the common life. Through these elements of his inner life, the
religious prays for souls, makes reparation for them and
reaches out to them in apostolic work; the preacher testifies by "work and example", while his spiritual life merits
for his apostolate many graces.

The Doctrinal Approach

The Dominican cannot pursue these contemplative
and apostolic objectives without constant study. If he
neglects it, he jeopardizes his vocation. It too must be
carried on in a contemplative spirit. The Constitutions
establish "the assiduous study of sacred truth" as a fundamental means for attaining the Order's ends. St. Dominic
wanted his friars to search for sacred truth chiefly in the
Holy Scriptures. He "often admonished and exhorted
the friars of the said Order by word and letter to study
constantly in the Old and New Testament." His Constitutions forbade the foundation of a priory without providing it with a professor as well as a prior. They incorporated an academic code for students, permitted the
brethren "to read, write, pray, sleep, and also, those who
wish, to stay up at night to study" in their cells, and instructed the master of novices to teach his charges "how
they ought to be so intent on study that day and night, at
home or on the road, they read or meditate something."

The study of sacred truth is the Dominican's primary preparation for preaching, but when obedience sends
him into activities other than preaching, he is then committed to the study of every area of truth which will make
his work for souls a success. The broadened apostolate
of today places on the friar the obligation of studying
and mastering any field of work into which he is sent.
He must constantly study its material, master its tech-
niques, learn its methods. Not only must Dominican

pastors, teachers, writers, missionaries, retreat masters, or nursing sisters remain up-to-date, mastering the advances in their special fields, but they must also never let their understanding of sacred doctrine become stale.

The busy priest might hold up his hands in dismay when considering these obligations, but remaining current is a matter of perseverance, rather than of extended and intense study. Many sisters and priests cannot find time for formal study, but they can keep their background-knowledge fresh and meaningful by an intelligent choice of books for daily spiritual reading, or, if they are engaged in teaching or other specialized works, by attention to recent bibliography and to technical journals of their field. Even the busiest Dominican, with a continual round from dawn to midnight—with classes to teach, lessons to prepare, papers to correct, or with Masses to celebrate, funerals to conduct, instructions to give, marriages to arrange, sick calls to make, as well as prayers to say—can in a minimum of two or three hours a week read a considerable number of sound theological or spiritual works during a year. Refectory reading, a traditional practice of monastic life, adds a welcome supplement to this basic diet of reading. Constant reading not only keeps the friar's own inner life vigorous but refreshes his knowledge and gives him a steady increase of material for his work in the pulpit and confessional.

Study and Contemplation

The most representative and saintly members of the Order, even its speculative theologians, have combined study and contemplation. St. Albert the Great outlined the contemplative approach to theology in his commentary on the *De mystica theologia* of Dionysius: "The method for one who teaches things divine is to gain by grace the truth of the divine doctrine he must hand on to others, because in every theological undertaking one ought to start with prayer."

William of Tocco, the first biographer of St. Thomas writes: "The entire life of Thomas was spent in prayer and contemplation, in writing, dictating, lecturing, preaching, or disputing."

Père Marie Joseph Lagrange, the Order's great biblical scholar, gave solid proof in his own life that the intimate bond between saintliness and learning, which distinguished Albert and Thomas, is still found in the modern Order. The remarks of a reviewer of Père Braun's, *The Work of Père Lagrange*, are most pertinent: "The most persistent impression that haunts the reader of this entire volume is that Père Braun intended to depict the lineaments of Lagrange the scholar, and wound up with the profile of a saint." We stop wondering why this should be so when we read the spiritual testament of this humble priest found among his papers after his death in 1938:

> I declare before God that it is my intention to die in the Holy Catholic Church to which I have always belonged with my whole heart and soul since the day of my baptism, and to die there faithful to my vows of poverty, chastity, and obedience, in the Order of St. Dominic. To that end, I commend myself to my good Savior Jesus, and to the prayers of his most holy Mother who has always been so good to me. I declare also most expressly that I submit to the judgment of the Apostolic See all that I have written. I believe that I can add that I have always had the intention in all my studies of contributing to the good, and by that I mean to the reign of Jesus Christ, to the honor of the Church, to the welfare of souls.

Only through such contemplative study, motivated by a deep love for God and souls, can the priest grasp the supernatural truths of the faith which he needs to propagate them zealously and clearly. This was the conviction of St. Thomas and the early friars. Humbert of Romans, his master general, reasoned this way in his commentary on the *Rule of St. Augustine*:

> The religious state is a state of contemplation. But things that are preached are gathered in contemplation, according to the words of Bl. Gregory, who says: "In contemplation they drink in what later they pour out in preaching." Therefore, it would seem that the religious state would have more that ought to be preached than the secular state, since it is more contemplative. Thus preaching befits it more because, not just by way of instruction but by way of contemplation as well, it possesses in abundance what it preaches.

The Balance of Dominican Life

The Order's spirituality is complex and made up of many elements, but they are unified in a single goal that is sublime. All its constituents lead to a contemplation which seeks to fructify in the apostolate. This evangelical vocation vitalizes all the other parts of Dominican life, carrying them upward to their highest development, which is exemplified by Christ and the Apostles. In his own life, St. Dominic demonstrated the unity amidst diversity which marks the spirituality he fashioned for his Order. Here is how Père Petitot describes the beautiful equilibrium of Dominic's life:

> That which especially characterizes him is the concord, the harmonious synthesis, of virtues, apparently the most contrary: gentleness with energy, love of study with love of action, genius for contemplation with the spirit of organization. Hence we have the figure of an apostle so happily balanced that, to find his equal, we must compare him with St. Bernard and St. Paul. From his birth to his death, St. Dominic followed one path, a marvelously straight trajectory, without turning back and without the slightest deviation of any sort. . . . . He was not a poet like Gregory Nazianzen or Francis of Assisi, nor was he a

writer like Augustine, but he was theologian, orator, apostle, ascetic, mystic, and saint.

The spiritual life of the Friars Preachers is delicately balanced and, for those who are less than saints, hard to live. If thrown off center its constituents destroy themselves—the sacerdotal element becomes "parochial", mired in local interests; the monastic element becomes "monkish," considering the apostolate a distraction; the doctrinal element becomes "bookish," having little to do with the salvation of souls; the apostolic element becomes "activistic," spending itself in feverish activity. To escape these extremes, the Dominican must nourish his zeal with a burning desire for Christ, must make contemplation primary in his life. His contemplation must center on Christ Crucified, thus engendering the apostolate. Père Regamey has crystallized this truth in these few words: "An apostolic message that has not been shaped in the sanctuary, the choir, and the cloister is never complete."

Dominican spirituality, born in the distant past, is not out of date. The current Constitutions are based on a thorough revision made in 1932, when Dominican law was brought into harmony with the Code of Canon Law. At that time ancient ordinances, prescriptions, and practices which had long been obsolete were combed out of the text, secondary practices were modified and adapted to modern life. Essential elements of the Dominican life and spirit, which cannot be changed without destroying the Order, were left unchanged. This work of "aggiornamento," the task of keeping the Order abreast of the times goes on constantly. The delegates sent to the general chapters (meeting at three-year intervals) bring to the highest legislative body of the Order the experience of priests from all over the world. Each chapter continues the work of its predecessor in making the Dominican life and apostolate more effective.

The priestly and apostolic qualities of the Order's spirituality do not render it unsuitable for the members of the Second and Third Orders. Dominican nuns, sisters, and tertiaries, marked in their souls with the characters of baptism and confirmation, bear the likeness of Christ's priesthood. They have the power to participate in Christian worship and the strength to extend its fruits to others. All members of the Order of Friars Preachers must be priestly and apostolic, thirsting for the salvation of souls.

ST. DOMINIC

Chapter II

THE DOMINICAN LIFE
is the
IMAGE OF
ST. DOMINIC

The Christian can most effectively learn how to live in holiness by studying the life of Christ, the Founder of Christianity. The Dominican can learn not only to become a holy Christian but also to live as a saintly religious by studying the ideas and life of St. Dominic, the Founder of the Order of Preachers. In his life the Friar Preacher can find the elements of the Order's spirituality. Pope Pius XI emphasized the importance of studying a Founder's life in his Apostolic letter *Unigenitus*:

> Above all we exhort religious to take as their model their own founder, their fatherly lawgiver, if they wish to have a sure and certain share in the graces which flow from their vocation. When the founder created his Order, what did he do but obey the divine inspiration? Therefore, the character which each one strove to impress upon his society must be retained by all its members if they are to remain faithful to his original ideal. As a good son, let each one devote himself heart and soul to honor his father and law-giver, to observe his commands and to drink in his spirit.

The Dominican must not only catch the spirit of St. Dominic, but, since he is seeking to learn the spirituality of a living organism, must also turn to the Rule of St. Augustine, the Constitutions, and the Order's history.

The Source of Dominican Spirituality

Everything positive in the Order's spiritual life traces back to Dominic, just as everything positive in the Church traces back to Christ. The present elements of Dominican spirituality are either the manifest intention of St. Dominic or valid developments of his ideas and plans. The doctrinal growth of the Order, brought about by Saints Albert and Thomas with the encouragement of Humbert of Romans in mid-thirteenth century, is an example of such a development. These holy men, basing themselves on the ideas and actions of St. Dominic, taught by word and example how an intense intellectuality, pursued for the love of Christ, can serve Christian truth and the spiritual life of the Dominican scholar.

Members of the Order should be well acquainted with St. Dominic and happy in his company, realizing how much he loves them. As their founder, he devoted the last precious years of his life to establishing the Order, visiting the first priories and monasteries, supervising, directing, encouraging, and teaching the friars and nuns. Divine Providence blessed him with a sympathetic heart and endowed him with the gift of directing his sons and guiding his daughters.

Most precious in learning the mind and spirituality of St. Dominic are the *Acts* of his canonization process, *The Little Book of the Origins of the Friars Preachers* by Jordan of Saxony (a brief history of the founder's life and the beginnings of the Order), and the primitive Constitutions. The first section of the Dominican Constitutions was borrowed by Dominic from the Constitutions of the Premonstratentians which he adapted by dropping passages, adding words, phrases, sentences, chapters, and especially a statement of purpose, to make them exactly suited to the Order's aims.

The witnesses in the canonization process of St. Dominic are divided into two groups. The larger numbered about three hundred men and women of the Toulouse region who had known him during the years before he founded the Order; the second group counted only nine friars who had been intimately associated with him during the last few years of his life. The relationship of these nine with the saint had been extremely close. All of them were part of the community at Bologna, his headquarters during his closing years, and they had been his traveling companions. They had every opportunity to see how he lived, prayed, ate, slept, did penance and suffered. They were the immediate objects of his solicitude and benefitted at first hand from his expert spiritual instruction. Their testimony gives us the best and the most detailed information about Dominic's heroic life. Both they and Jordan of Saxony had walked with him, prayed with him, nursed him in sickness, buried him, worked for his canonization, and first celebrated his feast. They captured Dominic's spirit, understood what he wanted for his Order, knew from his words and example how a friar preacher was to sanctify himself. We shall constantly quote these witnesses and let them tell us what they know about Dominic and the Order's genius and spirit.

The witnesses in southern France are somewhat disappointing. Though their evidence dovetails with that of the priests at Bologna, it is poor in detail. In one particular way, however, what they say surpasses what the men of Bologna said. Among the three hundred were three women. These ladies gave information that the male witnesses of both places never thought to give.

Willelma, the wife of Elias Martin, said she had known Dominic very well. She had made hairshirts for him and fed him more than two hundred times during those years in France. When he stopped at her house, she prepared lunch for him. At these times she noticed that he never ate more than a little bread and what would amount to the yolks of two eggs, or the fourth-part of a fish. When he took wine, he drank from glass that contained three-fourths water. Willelma gives us precious details, therefore, about his penitential diet.

Nogueza confirmed what Willelma had said. She never provided food for St. Dominic, but she also had made hairshirts for him. Beceda, who was a nun of the Holy Cross when she gave her testimony, likewise had sewn hairshirts for the Saint and had given him lunch. She described the same eating habits as Willelma. But she tells us something more. Often she provided a place of rest for Dominic. Always, the next morning, the bed was exactly as she had made it, undisturbed and un-rumpled. It had not been slept in. When Dominic stayed in her house, she would peep into his room and see him standing or kneeling in prayer. When he did sleep he would lay on the floor, and then she would tip-toe in and throw a blanket over him. A short time later she would look again, and he would be standing or kneeling in prayer once again. The solicitude of these three ladies for the holy man, the way they took care of him, demonstrated their love for him. He possessed a quality that won the confidence of women. They loved and trusted him.

Important information about St. Dominic also comes to us from a little treatise entitled: *The Nine Ways of Prayer of St. Dominic*. It was written by an anonymous author, probably at Bologna, sometime between 1260 and 1280. He had not known Dominic personally but culled his information from people who had reliable information about the Saint, among them probably Sister Cecilia who had received the Dominican habit from him at Rome in 1221. Later Jordan of Saxony had transferred her to the monastery of St. Agnes, Bologna, so that she could help train the community of Bl. Diana in the Order's life. The *Nine Ways* testifies to the eminent holiness of the Saint, showing something of his intimate life and intense love for God.

Sister Cecilia was indirectly responsible for another document called *The Miracles of Sister Cecilia* (though it is the miracles of St. Dominic that it records). In the community at Bologna, she often entertained the sisters with her reminiscences about the founder. Another sister wrote down these memories just as they fell from her lips. Therefore they lack the coherence of a biography, pay little attention to chronology, and are at times faulty in detail. But quite unconsciously Cecilia had woven into her narrative little details that tell us much about the traits of the Saint. It is these asides, as it were, that are very valuable. We see how Dominic began the monastery at San Sisto, how he prepared it for the occupancy of the nuns, how he persuaded them to transfer to it, to adopt a stricter way of life, and to take the vows of the Order of Preachers. After he had enclosed them and fixed the grill, he went every evening with a group of friars from Santa Sabina, a half-hour's walk, to instruct and form the nuns. These nightly conferences, spoken after he had ended a busy day of preaching and working in the city, bear witness to his abiding concern for his daughters. There is also an unsuspected side to his zeal. As he makes his apostolic rounds of Rome, we see him visiting, encouraging, and instructing the women recluses who at that time lived solitary lives in little cells built here and there into the city walls.

St. Dominic's Physical Features

Of all those who knew the founder, Sister Cecilia alone describes his physical characteristics and appearance. At the very end of *The Miracles* there is a fine verbal portrait of St. Dominic. Modern information helps to substantiate what she said. After World War II, Pope Pius XII authorized the Dominicans of Bologna to have the relics of the founder examined. During the war they had dismantled the tomb and placed it with the wooden casket containing the relics deep in the basement and covered them over with sandbags. After the war, with the Pope's permission, the Provincial of Lombardy had the relics examined by X-ray. He was not permitted to open the casket, but photographs from many angles were taken. Almost all the bones are still there after more than seven hundred years. Doctors and anthopologists were able to study them and give an accurate description of the skeleton and physical characteristics of St. Dominic. The Pope was so pleased with the results that he allowed the opening of the separate reliquary containing the head of the Saint so it could be examined more carefully.

For a long time historians did not think very highly of Sister Cecilia's memoirs. Their reasoning was that she was too old when she dictated them; she must have exaggerated all that she said; much of what she said seemed far-fetched; she must have given her imagination free play. But the study of the relics gave the lie to these doubts, at least so far as what she said about St. Dominic's appearance. Her description is proved reliable by the scientific examination. She said he was of medium height— the measurements show that he was five feet six inches tall. She said, "his figure was supple; his face handsome and somewhat ruddy; his hair and beard blond with a reddish tinge. He was not a bit bald, though here and there in his hair there was a touch of gray." At the bottom of the reliquary, the examiners found some shreds of St. Dominic's hair. It was exactly the color that Cecilia had said it was. "From his brow and eyes," she continued, "there came a radiant splendor which won the respect and admiration of all; his eyes were large and beautiful." St. Dominic's remains show large eye-sockets that are widely placed, confirming the physical description of Cecilia. With the scientific measurements and Cecilia's description an artist has reconstructed an image of St. Dominic. At least in size, shape, and proportion it conforms to life. Cecilia added: "His hands were long and handsome and his voice powerful and sonorous, and he was always joyous and smiling, except when moved with compassion at the affliction of his neighbors." There are very few saints of so long ago whose personal appearance is so well described.

His Spiritual Characteristics

However, we are more interested in St. Dominic's spiritual characteristics. Here also we are very fortunate. One of his outstanding characteristics was his priestliness. He manifests this trait at every moment of his life; we are almost tempted to say he was born a priest. As a boy of seven he began his formal education under the tutelage of an uncle who was a priest. His education was not that of a boy who would some day take up the sword and ride off to war; from the first, it was a priestly education. He learned Latin, chant, and liturgy. Then he enrolled at the cathedral school of Palencia. Here Dominic's ardent love for the teachings of the Church manifested itself. He could not study them enough. After a solid course in philosophy, he hastened on to theology and spent four years learning it. This is usual for priests today, but five centuries ago four years of theology was exceptional. He could not learn the doctrines of the faith fast enough to suit himself. He studied long into the night. In the margins of his books were the many notes he had written.

As canon of the cathedral chapter at Osma, where he made profession soon after his ordination to the priesthood, Dominic continued his studies. But now they were more the study of the contemplative priest, lovingly seeking to penetrate the truths of the faith with the assistance of the gifts of wisdom and understanding, under the guidance of the Holy Spirit. The doctrines of revelation had penetrated to the very core of Dominic's spiritual fibre before he became an apostle. When he was ready for this next step in his life, divine guidance carried him to southern France where he spent twelve years of his life, from 1205 to 1217, defending and preaching the faith. It is not surprising that when he founded his Order he made ample provision for his friars to learn and to love the doctrine they were to preach.

St. Dominic's love for the truths of the faith nourished in him a deep love for Our Divine Lord, the Image of God the Father, the Wisdom of God, the personification of all the mysteries and doctrines of the Church. We cannot love our faith without loving Christ. The famous Dominican mystic, Bl. Henry Suso, whose *Little Book of Holy Wisdom* is one of the finest pieces of western mysticism, constantly refers to Our Lord as the Holy Wisdom.

St. Dominic's love for Christ appears in his prayer. According to Jordan of Saxony, " he gave the day to his neighbor, the nights to God." He spent all night in church praying. There he found the altar and the Blessed Sacrament. If Dominic grew weary, Jordan tells us, he would lean against the altar; against his Lord, represented by the altar.

The founder had a profound devotion to the Mass, celebrating it every day; when possible, singing it. Invariably he was so moved by the sacred mystery taking place before him, that the tears flowed down his cheeks. Little wonder that he made the Order of Preachers a liturgical order. One of the great means he set for the realization of the Order's end is the solemn chanting of the Divine Office; for lay brothers, Sisters and tertiaries, the Little Office of the Blessed Mother. The Office flows from the Mass, the climax of the liturgy. The Mass is the diamond, the Office is its setting. The hours of the Office lead to the Mass and follow from the Mass; preparing for it and bringing us its fruits the rest of the day.

Because he loved Christ, St. Dominic constantly carried the Gospel of St. Matthew and the Epistles of St. Paul. We, with our compact New Testaments, might be tempted to say, "Well, that was not much of a feat, why didn't he carry the whole Bible?" We can do that without any trouble, but it was a different problem in those days of handwritten books. Manuscripts were bulky and expensive. If they were small, the handwriting had to be almost microscopic. Dominic carried the books he loved best, the ones that spoke most clearly to him of Our Divine Savior. Jordan of Saxony says that he read these works so much that he practically knew them by heart.

Dominic's devotion to Our Lord carried his soul into the depths of the mystery of the Passion. Many of the witnesses, both at Toulouse and Bologna, testify that he spent almost all the night in prayer. During this prayer, he was so moved that he often prayed aloud. "How do you know this?" some of the witnesses were asked. Rudolph of Faenza replied: "Well, I know it because I wanted to see what he did in the church at night, so I hid myself in the church behind a pillar and I heard him." He was praying and making reparation for sinners: "O Lord, have mercy on Thy people . . . what is to become of sinners?" His soul, writes Jordan, "was a sanctuary of compassion" where "he offered God all human misery." He would interrupt his petitions to take the discipline.

His desire for reparation dictated a scanty menu. When the brethren had two courses for dinner, he was satisfied with one. He would always finish eating before the others, and then, as he listened to the reader, would often be overcome by fatigue and doze. Besides his scanty food, his sleepless nights, his use of the hairshirt, Dominic wore a chain around his waist. Rudolph of Faenza found it at his death and gave it to Jordan. These austerities were prompted by his desire to participate in the Passion of Christ, to contribute his share to the redemption of souls. How he loved souls. They were members of the Mystical Body of Christ, redeemed by his Precious Blood. It is impossible to love Christ deeply without loving souls. If we do not love them, we cannot work for their salvation and our love for Christ will be superficial and shallow. St. Dominic knew that, in the words of Mary at Fatima, "Many souls were going to hell because there was no one to make sacrifices for them." The founder kept solemn and solitary nightly vigils, praying for the success of the apostolate which he zealously and vigorously pursued during the day.

St. Dominic wanted to become a missionary, seeking for the salvation of souls. During his last years, after he had founded the Order, he was always talking about going to preach to the pagans. When he first left Spain in the company of the Bishop of Osma, going to Denmark to escort to Spain a princess who was destined to marry the King's son, they reached the North at a time when the Archbishop of Lund was organizing an intense missionary endeavor in the Baltic area. Dominic and his bishop learned about the pagan peoples of Prussia, Lithuania, and Esthonia from the reports coming back to Denmark from the East. Dominic never forgot these pagans. He remembered also the Moors in his native Spain, the Cuman Tartars in Hungary. He promised William of Montferrat, a young disciple, that they would go together to the missions after the Order was well organized. He began to grow a beard with this in mind. Organizing the Order took longer than Dominic expected, and he was never able to become a missionary. But he communicated his zeal to his children. William of Montferrat was one of the first friars to preach to the Saracens of Palestine. Our Order has always been a great missionary Order. Today about twenty percent of its members are in the foreign mission field.

Those who knew Dominic tell us that he wanted to give his life for souls, if necessary. With courage he traveled through the Albigensian country. At times he knew

his enemies were planning to kill him, yet he continued
on his way. Once they took him, but seeing that he offered no resistance, they asked: "What would you have
done, had we carried out our plans?" "I would have begged you to put me to death in the slowest possible way,
to cut me to pieces bit by bit so my martyrdom would be
prolonged for the good of souls." Realizing how much
he wanted martyrdom, they did not kill him. He was a
martyr by desire.

Dominic's compassion for people made him willing,
as a student at Palencia, to sell his books to feed the hungry. When he first came into Toulouse on his way to
Denmark, he lodged with an innkeeper who was a heretic.
Though Dominic had traveled all day long across an un-
familiar country, he spent his first night in that new land
persuading and converting his host. Finally, after years of
work in the Albigensian lands, he realized he could not
save all these souls alone. The idea of founding an order of preachers gradually grew in his mind.

As a good priest, St. Dominic was firm in correcting.
This might seem a peculiar illustration of priestliness, but
correction is a great charity to an erring soul. Rudolph of
Faenza describes this quality of Dominic:

> He was always cheerful and pleasant, a com-
> forter of the brethren. He was patient, merci-
> ful, and kind. If he saw a brother breaking any
> rule, he would pass by as though he had not seen
> it. But afterward he would, with a mild expres-
> sion and kind word, say, "Brother, you must con-
> fess your fault." With his gentle words he in-
> duced all to confess and repent.

He rigorously punished transgressors, but they went away
consoled because of his humble attitude. He made the
necessary correction with firmness, with an adequate penance, but knowing how delicately a soul must be treated,
he did not break the man's spirit. Paul of Venice testified:

He rigidly and perfectly kept the rule himself and exhorted and commanded the brethren to do the same, and he strictly punished offenders. Yet he reproved them with such patience and kindness that no one was ever upset or rebellious because of the correction.

As a saintly priest, St. Dominic excelled in giving advice, in counselling and consoling. The sources mention this many times. Stephen of Spain, who was still a student at the University when Dominic first came to Bologna and clothed him in the habit can testify for all:

Both the brethren and others found Brother Dominic to be the best possible comforter when they were troubled with temptations. He knew this fact because when he first entered religion and was a novice he had many temptations. But he was put completely at ease by the preaching and counselling of St. Dominic. Many other novices told him that they had had the same experience with Dominic. The witness never saw any man who was more zealous to strengthen the Order, to preserve the Rule, and to comfort the brethren. He did not think Dominic would ever have a comparable successor in these qualities.

The secret source of Dominic's priestly strength was his great reliance on Divine Providence. His years of work among the Albigenses were apparently, by human standards, not very fruitful. There were conversions, but there is no record of mass conversions. They did not come by the thousands and the tens of thousands, as some of the older lives say. Trusting in Divine Providence Dominic was willing to continue for many years in the face of a very difficult apostolate. He kept working and hoping for the harvest. It did not come in southern France, but he gathered it when he founded the Order. His Order is still reaping the benefit of his trust. When Dominic had only sixteen brethren, he scattered them, contrary to the advice of the Bishop of Toulouse and Count Simon de Montfort. He sent them to Paris, Spain, and Rome, despite the human prudence of his friends. They thought he was tearing down what he had laboriously built, destroying the Order he had just founded. But he had the supernatural prudence that comes from the Holy Spirit. "Seed rots when it is hoarded, bears fruit when it is sown." When he came to Paris, just two years later, instead of the original eight, he found thirty. A few years more and his disciples were counted by the thousands.

The very fact that Dominic was willing to found a Mendicant Order, one that owned no property and had no revenues, indicates his mighty trust in Divine Providence. He relied on the free-will offerings the faithful would give him. He so believed in God's help, that he did not want the brethren to store up more food than they needed for a day. That is why they sometimes went hungry. But his faith was rewarded, more than once by the miracle of the loaves. Both in Bologna and in Rome there were days when the early friars, unknown newcomers, did not get enough from their begging tours. Then they found a bare refectory. There was nothing to place before them. But the Founder had them offer the grace and take their places just the same. At Rome the angels came and distributed a loaf of bread to each friar. This was the answer of Providence to Dominic's trust. Some twenty years after his death, the Order made the law less severe. The friars were now allowed to store up enough for a year. Did the friars lack the trust of their Father? Or had the Order grown too large all of a sudden? By the end of the thirteenth century, too, the charity of the people had grown noticeably cooler.

The Imitation of St. Dominic

St. Dominic's priestliness shines in his love for the doctrines of the Church, his personal love for Our Lord in the Mass and the Blessed Sacrament, his penances in imitation of the Suffering Christ, his love for souls, his ability to give advice and counsel, his trust in Divine Providence. Priestliness is his chief characteristic. Dominican laybrothers, nuns, sisters, and tertiaries might say, "How can we follow him in this?" "How can we imitate his priestliness?" Baptism stamped the Christian character on their souls, the character of Christ, the Eternal Priest. It is a sharing in His priesthood, enabling them to share in the priestly worship of the Church. In this sense all Dominicans can live their lives in a priestly manner, imitating the priestliness of their Founder—his love for the doctrines of the Church, for the suffering Christ, for the Mass and Blessed Sacrament, for souls, and his reliance on Providence.

All Dominicans should nourish a tender devotion to their founder. It does not matter that they find another saint more effective in answering prayers. We do not pray, primarily, to get answers, at least, not material answers. From St. Dominic we shall receive spiritual answers: the ability to understand the Dominican life, to live it well and to be zealous for souls.

Dominicans should go to Dominic because he is a priest and remains one for all eternity. In heaven, he keeps the priestly outlook, still wants to help souls, can still counsel and give advice. When we are troubled we go to the priest. Dominicans, go to Dominic, the priest. Go to him because he is also your father. Parents in heaven see their children on earth, know their needs and difficulties, and can help them. A spiritual relationship binds St. Dominic to his children. The vows of the religious and the promise of the tertiary make them his sons and daughters. Having a claim on him, they should remind him of that fact. They should go to him, asking for spiritual blessings, for the grace of contemplation, for the grace to live their Dominican life in a holy way. They should remind him that he promised to answer. When the friars came sorrowfully to his deathbed, recommending themselves to his prayers, his reassuring words were: "Where I am going, I will be of more use to you than I have ever been on earth." Fulfill, O Father, what thou hast said. . . .

ST. DOMINIC AT MENTAL PRAYER

Chapter III

DOMINICAN LIFE
is
CONTEMPLATIVE

The Christian is the image of Christ. The Dominican is the image of St. Dominic. As a canon of Osma, before he became an apostle, he was a contemplative. Here is how Jordan of Saxony describes these years at Osma: "Day and night he frequented the church, giving himself without interruption to prayer. Redeeming the time by contemplation, he scarcely left the walls of the monastery." Then St. Dominic went into southern France to begin his years of ceasely apostolic activity. He became an apostle but did not stop being a contemplative. Abbot William Peter of St. Paul's monastery in Toulouse, who had known Dominic personally, testified that he had never seen anyone pray or weep so much. Dominic's prayer was so intense that it forced him to pray aloud: "O Lord, have mercy on Thy people . . . what is to become of sinners?"

The Dominican Order is Contemplative

St. Dominic founded an Order that is contemplative in all its branches—the First Order, Second Order, Third Order Conventual, and the Third Order of Tertiaries. Any Dominican who is not eager to become a contemplative is falling short in his Dominican spirit.

Some people hold that it is impossible to unite the contemplative and active lives, because each of these lives is so engrossing. The life of prayer claims all the attention of a person; activity claims all his attention also. When Dominic founded the Friars Preachers, some people said it was impossible to have an Order that combined both features. They knew only two kinds of Order. There were the contemplative Benedictines, Cistercians, Carthusians, Premonstratentians, and so forth. They led the life of prayer. Not that they never left the cloister, but the vow of stability bound them to one monastery for their whole life. The active Orders were strictly active, the Knights Templars, Knights of St. John, Teutonic Knights, the Orders of Ransom, and Orders that took care of pilgrims and the sick, running inns and hospitals. Only the Canons Regular, leading the contemplative life, undertook a limited, parochial ministry.

St. Dominic founded a new kind of Order, one that pursued an intense life of prayer and yet embraced a general apostolic activity. He personally demonstrated that it is possible to be a contemplative of the highest type and also a zealous apostle. But these two lives can be united only when the apostle gives primacy to contemplation. It must be Christian contemplation, pondering the mysteries of our redemption—Christ's desire to save all souls, his death on the Cross for the redemption of sinners, the Father's love in sending Christ to us. That type of prayer becomes apostolic; the contemplative seeks the salvation of his neighbor, because, like the early Christians, when he "sees his neighbor, he sees God."

St. Dominic prayed in that way. Jordan of Saxony writes: "He shared the daytime with his neighbor, but the night he dedicated to God." He spent so much of his night in prayer, that he hardly needed a bed. In fact, his friars testified that he never had a bed of his own. When he slept, he slept in a chair, on the floor, leaning against the altar, or dozed at table. At night he prayed as long as his body could endure it. When sleep overpowered him, he rested his head, like the patriach Jacob, upon a stone. After a short rest, Jordan notes, he would rouse his spirit and renew his fervent prayer. He was first and foremost a contemplative, and his children must be contemplatives.

Contemplation is the chief purpose of the Order. The Dominican does not contemplate because he wants to become an apostle. That would make it a means to an end. Contemplation *is* so superior, that it cannot be subordinated to anything lesser. The Dominican seeks contemplation for its own sake, because contemplation unites him to God. "Seek first the kingdom of God and his justice, and all these things shall be given to you besides" (Matt. 6:33).

Contemplation—the Source of the Apostolate

When a friar prays, he hopes his prayer will become deep and profound, filling his own soul with such grace and spiritual energy that they will overflow on the souls of others. The image of his life is a deep well. It fills slowly until its pure water reaches the top; then the water runs over the brim and begins to irrigate the whole countryside. The well never empties itself in watering the fields, but gives of its abundance. The Dominican must sanctify himself before he can go out to help his neighbor. The end of the Order, in all branches, is a contemplation that fructifies in the apostolate. A Dominican's life is a life hidden in God with Christ, lived in the solitude and silence of the religious house. There he dwells alone with God while his exterior activity is the voice of cloistered silence.

The Dominican goes into the pulpit, the classroom, or the sick-room because obedience sends him, because his apostolic yearning to help souls impels him to go. He does not undertake these works through natural eagerness to exercise his talents, or to fulfill his personality. Of course this does not mean that if a priest likes to preach, he must no longer delight in it; nor if he loves teaching, that he must curb the joy he experiences. It means only that his motive in going out to work is not personal gratifications but the glory of God and the good of neighbor.

All other motives urging him onward to works of the apostolic life are less worthy. With his usual acuteness, St. Thomas describes the failure of most religious who plunge into the apostolate: "They are led to engage in external works rather from the weariness which they feel for the contemplative life, than from a desire to attain to the fulness of divine love" (*De perf. vitae sp.*, c. 23). "There are some who are deprived of freedom for divine contemplation and immersed in secular affairs willingly or without regret; in these persons very little or no charity is evident" (*De carit.*, a. 11, ad 6).

But Thomas finds not only activists weary with the contemplative life, but also selfish contemplatives. "They so enjoy divine contemplation," he writes, "that they do not want to forsake it, even to consecrate themselves to the service of God by saving their neighbor" (*De carit.*, a. 11, ad 6).

The true Dominican resembles neither of these types. If his neighbor did not need him, he would stay in his religious house with God, but because of his neighbor's dire necessity, he longs to give him the fruits of his own interior life. There is an intimate connection between his prayer and his apostolic yearnings. This distinguishes him from the purely contemplative monk who may go forth out of obedience, as did St. Bernard, to work for the salvation of his neighbor. The Dominican, seeing God in his neighbor, is constrained by the impetus of his own contemplation to bring that neighbor to God. Therefore, as St. Thomas observes:

 . . . at the expense of his much loved contemplation, he devotes himself, for God's sake, to his neighbor's salvation. Hence, it is a proof of a greater perfection of charity to be willing, for the love of God and neighbor, to work for the salvation of others, even though, by so doing, contemplation be somewhat impaired, than to cling so closely to the sweetness of contemplation as to be unwilling to sacrifice it, even for the salvation of others (*De perf. vitae sp.*, c. 23).

Tormented by a passion for souls, the Dominican brings them a message that has been matured in silent prayer before God, that has "been shaped in the sanctuary, the choir, and the cloister."

This eminent ideal, this search for contemplation that fructifies in the apostolate, has been expressed concretely in the oldest, the simplest, and the most beautiful Dominican rule of conduct. It comes directly from the practice of St. Dominic. The canonization witnesses tell us that he spoke only with God or of God. We shall let Stephen speak for them all:

> It was his custom to speak always of God or with God whether he was in or outside the priory or on a journey. He strongly urged the brethren to act in the same way and he had this placed in the Constitutions.

Speaking thus of God, in conversation or in sermons, Dominic's contemplation spilled over the brim of his prayerful soul to the sanctification of those who heard him.

The Dominican saints learned this lesson from their father. They also spoke with God and of God. Bl. Raymond of Capua writes this about St. Catherine of Siena:

> . . . if she had intelligent people to talk to, she could have gone on talking to them about God for a hundred days and nights without stopping for food or drink. She never got tired talking about God. On the contrary, as time went on, she seemed to grow ever more lively and enthusiastic. Again and again she has told me she knew of no greater consolation in life than talking and arguing about God with people of understanding. And anyone who ever worked with her can vouch for this from personal experience.

Raymond goes on for another page, telling how he fell asleep once when Catherine was talking to him about God. She awoke him with a rebuke: "Is this all you care about the salvation of your soul?"

St. Thomas gave theological expression to the Order's motto when he said that an apostolic religious must "con-

template and give to others the fruit of his contemplation"
(*Summa theol.*, II—II, p. 188, a. 6). The Dominican apostle must "speak with God or of God."

Contemplation—Inherent in Dominican Life

Is it possible to prove that the Order is contemplative? This can be done by first considering the kind of
Order St. Dominic founded: an Order of Canons Regular.
The bull of confirmation issued by Pope Honorius III on
December 22, 1216 began with the words *Religiosam
vitam.* Hundreds of similar bulls open with the same
words and with the same general content. They vary in
detail but are always given in favor of chapters of canons
regular. The chief duty of the canons was contemplative
—the worship of the Holy Trinity. The canons existed to
carry out the divine worship of the Church in a solemn
manner. They were attached to the cathedrals precisely
for that purpose: to worship God officially, to participate in the solemn Mass, to chant the Divine Office in
the name of the Church. They were officially "pray-ers".
The issuance of the *Religiosam vitam* by Pope Honorius
served notice on the Friars Preachers that they were Canons Regular and that their chief function was to worship
God in a contemplative way.

St. Dominic also adopted the monastic observances—
the community life, cloister, silence, austerities of fasting
and abstinence, bowings during the Office and Mass,
venias, the scapular—from the contemplative Orders. The
first part of the primitive Constitutions was almost ex-
clusively devoted to these things. The Founder took them
from the Premonstratentians, who borrowed them from the
Cistercians, a most strict, contemplative Order. Dominican
nuns and sisters have taken these observances from the
fathers. Tertiaries perform the bows when they recite the
Office during their meetings. Even in their private recita-
tions, the members of the Order should bow their heads
reverently at the *Gloria Patri.* The observances are a sign
to the friar that he must be a contemplative.

The second part of the early Constitutions also clearly demonstrates the contemplative character of the Order. This part, governing preaching, study, and apostolate, held before friars going out to preach a vivid portrait of their contemplative apostolic career:

> They shall receive a blessing and then go forth as men desirous of their own salvation and the salvation of others. Let them bear themselves with religious decorum as men of the Gospel, treading in the footsteps of their Savior and speaking with God or about God to themselves and their neighbor. . . .

The present Constitutions prescribe the same ideals, repeating the words of 1220:

> It is known that our Order was founded from the beginning for the express purpose of preaching and the salvation of souls. . . .
>
> This end we ought to pursue, preaching and teaching from the abundance and fulness of contemplation, after the example of our most holy father Dominic, who used to speak only with God or of God to the great benefit of souls.
>
> The means set by that most holy patriach for the attainment of that end are, besides the three solemn vows of obedience, chastity, and poverty, regular life with its monastic observances, the solemn recitation of the Office, and the assiduous study of sacred truth. Among us these means cannot be abolished or substantially altered, though it is permissible (the vows, of course, excepted) to temper them somewhat, opportunely, so that they might be more suited for a facile reaching of the end and possess greater efficacy and be more suited for a more expedite attainment of the end.

The *Rule of St. Augustine*, chosen by St. Dominic as best suited for his purposes in founding the Order, likewise imposes the duty of contemplation. It opens with a statement, in different words, of the Order's great intention to speak only "with God or of God." "Before all things, dear brethren, love God and after him your neigh-

bor." These words are a trumpet call to contemplation.
The Rule first ascends to the very throne of God to look
on him in loving contemplation; then it descends, bringing his love to souls. Humbert of the Romans, fifth master
general, makes a beautiful application of these words
to the Dominican preacher in his comment on the Rule:

> It is the duty of the preacher at times to devote
> himself to contemplating the things of God; at
> times, however, to exert himself in action for his
> neighbor. The love of God raises him up to the
> first; the love of neighbor carries him down to the
> second . . . but because each one owes more to
> himself than to his neighbor, he must give him-
> self more to the quiet of the contemplative life
> than to the works of the active, like the workers
> of Solomon, who rested more than they worked.
> He must seek the things of God more than he
> seeks the things of his neighbor, and must preach
> more to himself than to others, preferring the love
> of God to the love of neighbor, because that is the
> first and the greatest commandment. Therefore,
> there is an order in these things and it is rightly
> written: "Before all things love God, and then
> the neighbor."

The words of the Rule illustrate the sublimity and spirituality of the Dominican vocation. Above all else, it urges
the fulfillment of the two great commandments: "Thou
shalt love the Lord thy God with thy whole heart, and
with thy whole soul, and with thy whole mind. This is
the greatest and the first commandment. And the second
is like it; thou shalt love thy neighbor as thyself" (Matt.
12:37-39).

Contemplation and Preaching

The contemplative character of the Order is demonstrated from the special end that St. Dominic established
—preaching for the salvation of souls. The primitive
Constitutions clearly state this purpose in their prologue:
"It is known that our Order was founded from the beginning for preaching and the salvation of souls." Spread-

ing the word of God for souls demands a contemplative life from the apostle. St. Peter clearly taught this truth when the first deacons were chosen. Pointing out the need for the new office, he spoke for the Twelve:

> It is not desirable that we should forsake the word of God and serve at tables. Therefore, brethren, select from among you seven men of good reputation, full of the Spirit and of wisdom, that we may put them in charge of this work. But we will devote ourselves to prayer and to the ministry of the word (Acts, 6:2-4).

He even wanted contemplation for the "active" deacons. They must be men "full of the Spirit and of wisdom."

St. Dominic, an apostle among the Albigenses, devoted himself "to prayer and the ministry of the word," giving "his day to his neighbor, his night to God." Humbert of the Romans, in his *Commentary* on the Rule shows how well the first sons of St. Dominic imitated their Founder:

> The state of a religious is the state of a contemplative. The things that are preached are learned in contemplation. Speaking of preachers the blessed Gregory said: "in contemplation they drink in the truths which later they pour out in their preaching." The office of the preacher is, on the one hand, to give himself to contemplating the things of God, and, on the other, to devote himself to activities on behalf of his neighbor. He must give himself to both the active and the contemplative lives. But since everyone is responsible first for himself, the preacher must devote himself much more to contemplation than to the works of the active life.

Contemplation in the Lives of Sisters and Tertiaries

All that we have said about contemplation applies equally to Dominican sisters. This is clear regarding the nuns of the Second Order, but the sisters of the Conventual Third Order are also committed to the Order's spiritual life. Dominican spirituality is the same, in its basic principles, for all members of the Order. No congregation of sisters or brothers can be affiliated with the Order unless the master general is satisfied that its constitutions and customs faithfully reflect the spirit of the Friars Preachers. A congregation enjoying such affiliation can be sure that the Order is satisfied with the contemplative character of its laws and customs. All parts of the Order, except the secular Third Order, follow the *Rule of St. Augustine.* Read regularly in the refectory, the Rule continually challenges the brethren with these words:

> Before all things, dear brethren, love God and after him your neighbor, because these are the principal commands which have been given to us. These, then, are the things which we command you who live in the monastery to observe: first, that you dwell together in unity in the monastery and have one mind and one heart in the Lord, for this is the reason why you have come together.

The Constitutions of the sisters, as those of the fathers, commit them to the contemplative life. The Friars Preachers were founded by St. Dominic for the sanctification of its members and the salvation of souls. The sisters "as true daughters of their holy Founder and Patriarch, must always remember this twofold object and strive with all their energy to attain it." The first emphasis is on their own salvation. The Order was founded to sanctify its members, to make them "perfect in charity." In the second place it seeks the salvation of souls. The principal and essential purpose of the Dominican in entering the religious life is to achieve his personal sanctification. This he does through the three vows of religion and by keeping the Rule and Constitutions. These guiding documents for Dominicans, together with the sisters' customary, oblige them to follow the contemplative monastic observances as they were set down in 1216 by St. Dominic.

The sisters also take the vows, follow their Constitutions, and keep the Rule. They wear the Order's habit with its scapular, the badge of a contemplative Order. They have the fasts and abstinences, the enclosure, community life, silence, the Office and all the many Dominican sacramentals which help to lead their souls to God.

Infused Contemplation—the Dominican Ideal

When St. Dominic placed contemplation before his children as the primary end of their lives, he intended infused contemplation. The thirteenth century did not know the distinction made by later spiritual writers between "infused" and "acquired" contemplation. The Founder did not rule out vocal prayer, mental prayer, or other kinds of active prayer. He practiced them himself and enjoined them as dispositive agents preparing for the higher types of prayer.

Comtemplation is primarily an act of the intellect, but it begins in love, an act of the will. When the soul loves God, it longs to be united to him. Ardent love for God leads to the contemplative act. Once the soul has found God in contemplation, its love, by a reciprocal process, is increased. In the presence of the one we love, we experience delight; this, in turn, leads to an increase of love. Contemplation, therefore, is a circular motion (*Summa theol.*, II—II, q. 180, a. 6). It begins in love of God; it leads to our gazing upon him; thus lost in our enjoyment of him, we learn to love him more intensely.

Some might object that infused contemplation is a gift of God; it cannot be acquired. God gives it to whom he pleases, when he pleases, and as much as he pleases. It is given when the Holy Spirit makes his Gifts, especially wisdom, knowledge, and understanding, active in the soul. Then the soul is made docile and readily responsive to the whisperings of the Spirit. If that is true; if contemplation is a gift of God; if we cannot acquire it by our own efforts, then how can we be true Domicans? Not everyone, and maybe only a few are given this gift. Of course, we do not know who has it or who does not have it. Sometimes a person may have it and not be aware of it himself. Or a soul may experience contemplation once, a few times, or frequently. So the difficulty remains, how can we be true to our vocation if here and now we are not contemplative? We are true to our calling if we live our contemplative vocation sincerely, if we try habitually to dispose ourselves for the higher prayer. This is required even of a person who enjoys the act of contemplation. It is an act and, therefore, transitory; it lasts for a time and then ceases. Even one so gifted must constantly be disposing himself, otherwise he will lose God's blessing.

Preparing for Contemplation

How can this be done? St. Thomas prescribes hearing, reading, meditating, and praying (*Summa theol.*, II—II, q. 180, a. 3 ad 4). A Dominican prepares for contemplation when he listens to sermons, when he reads spiritual books, when he prays mentally or vocally. Chanting Office in choir, during which the soul savors the sacred texts and listens to the whispering of the Invisible Teacher, was the means preferred by St. Dominic to dispose his children for contemplation.

The Dominican should constantly and humbly beg God for this gift. It is a higher grace directly conducive to sanctity and may, therefore, be legitimately desired. Our Lord, in the words spoken to the woman who had come to Jacob's well to draw water, encourages us to ask for the contemplative graces: "If thou didst know the gift of God, and who it is who says to thee, 'Give me to drink,' thou perhaps wouldst have asked of him, and he would have given thee living water" (John, 4:10). The Book of Wisdom teaches that such prayer made humbly and perseveringly can expect an answer: "I called upon God and the spirit of wisdom came upon me" (Wisd., 7:7). The soul prays humbly for this grace when it realizes that it is God's gift and the answer depends on his Will. He may not answer this prayer in the present life, or he may answer it later when the soul has done more to dispose itself. He may answer it only once, or he may answer it more abundantly. We may pray for contemplation without presumption, because infused contemplation is the normal flowering of the life of grace, which should continue developing until it reaches its maturity in contemplation. Should this not take place, it will occur in eternity, following the purifications of purgatory. When trials and sufferings come into his life, the religious should never complain; rather he should welcome them as purifications which will cleanse his soul, show him his weakness, and draw him gradually toward union with God. Many souls lose all the purgative value of sufferings when they rebel or fall into self pity.

The Dominican who appreciates the Divine generosity, will beg God incessantly for the higher spiritual gifts. However, this prayer will be presumptuous if it is not matched by unending, vigorous efforts on his part to do everything possible to dispose himself for the higher graces. Utmost fidelity to the prayer and the duties of his religious life are the providential means given to the religious to accomplish this work. Deliberate neglect or habitual infidelity to religious duties will nullify all efforts in begging of God the higher forms of prayer.

If the Dominican prays for the grace of contemplation, then he must be ready to pay the price. No one can become a contemplative unless he is willing to die totally to self. Everything in the Order's religious life prepares its members to die to self and live in God. The friar begins to die to self when he commences to live his religious life earnestly; when he begins to mortify, put to death, his own will, desires, likes and dislikes. He must even learn to put aside, on many occasions, his own opinions. If he is faithful to the monastic observances, silence, fasts, abstinence, and the many other things that are so insignificant in themselves, he dies to self. Such fidelity to minutiae prepares him for contemplation by clearing away the obstacles, chiefly self-will and personal vice, which impede it and by requiring the practice of the virtues which promote it, such as obedience, patience, perseverance and charity.

The Dominican lives in God when he enters whole-
heartedly into liturgical prayer, study, and the apostolate. The liturgy and loving study of sacred truth place
him in direct contact with God, the object of contemplation. The apostolate carries fruits of contemplation to
souls. Nothing in the Order's spiritual scheme is useless.
Every element in its spirituality is essentially integrated
in a master plan for the sanctification of the Dominican
and the salvation of souls.

The Order's life, Rule, Constitutions, and customs are
grand. They are grand in design, grand in purpose, grand
in their effect. A Dominican should live them as well as
he can, deeply lamenting when he fails. He should per-
severe in keeping his Rule and Constitutions all the days
of his life, never yielding to discouragement. Only God
knows why he gives contemplation to some and not to
others; why he gives it early or late; why he gives it oc-
casionally or frequently. St. Augustine teaches that this
is a mystery, that if we do not wish to err, we should not
inquire. Rather the soul should turn inward to scrutinize
its own conduct, to see where it is still failing in complete
fidelity to grace. If God gives it the graces of contemplation, it must respond with great gratitude and love.

If the friar does all he can to make himself ready
for contemplation, he will certainly work most effectively
for the sanctification of his soul. Only failure on his
part to pursue the ends of the Order, to use the means
it provides, or to use them in proper balance, stand as
obstacles to contemplation. Preaching, teaching, nursing,
and the vast variety of work done by the Order in the
modern world do not prevent a Dominican from aspiring
to be, or becoming, a contemplative.

The Order produces contemplatives and has them
at the present day. Perhaps the reader may not know of
any, but there are many. The saints of the Order exemplify the beautiful balance of Dominican spirituality, the
perfect blend of contemplation and apostolicity. They
have been among the greatest contemplatives of the

Church: St. Dominic, St. Thomas Aquinas, St. Catherine of Siena, St. Vincent Ferrer, yet they have been zealous apostles. The pages of Dominican history are sprinkled liberally with great souls who have become saints in the Dominican way, following their rule with utmost fidelity, working faithfully for the good of souls.

ST. DOMINIC PREACHING

Chapter IV

DOMINICAN LIFE

is

APOSTOLIC

The general end of the Dominican Order is the sanctification of its members through contemplation; its special end is the salvation of souls through preaching. These two ends are not contradictory; in fact, they are one. The second implies the first. Preaching is the fruit of the life of prayer. Through contemplation the Dominican loves God so much that he must love his neighbor and become an apostle. He cannot rest until he proclaims God's glory to the whole world.

Contemplation Makes the Apostle

The Order's vocation is sublime. It enables the friar to fulfill the two supreme precepts of the law: "Thou shalt love the Lord thy God with thy whole heart, and with thy whole soul, and with thy whole mind. This is the greatest and the first commandment. And the second is like it; thou shalt love thy neighbor as thyself" (Matt. 22: 37-39). It is God first, and then the neighbor.

This order of love is seen very well in the life of St. Catherine of Siena. She first became a contemplative, then an apostle. In the first part of his life of Catherine, Bl. Raymond of Capua describes her prayer life—how she learned to love God by retiring from the world, even

as she continued living at home with her family. She had
her little cell and was happy in her life of prayer with
God, content to continue so until her death. But then
Our Lord appeared to her, telling her that she would
become an apostle:

> Your heart will burn so strongly for the salvation
> of your fellow men that you will forget your sex
> and you will change your present way of life.
> You will not avoid the company of men and
> women as you do now, but for the salvation of
> their souls you will take upon yourself every
> kind of labor.

Later in his volume Raymond relates how this happened. After Catherine reached the heights of the mystical life and had received the grace of spiritual marriage,
the Lord brought her out of her retirement, compelling
her almost, to become an apostle, to have dealings with
other people, yet not depriving her of His company: "Go,
it is dinner time and the rest of the family is about to sit
down at the table. Go and be with them and then come
back to Me." Catherine protested: "No, Lord, it is far
from the immense perfection of your goodness to order
me or anybody thus to be in any way separated from Thy
goodness." To this protest Our Lord replied:

> Be quiet, sweetest daughter. It is necessary for
> you to fulfill every duty so that, with my grace,
> you may assist others as well as yourself. I have
> no intention of cutting you off from me. On the
> contrary, I wish to bind you more closely to my-
> self by means of love of neighbor . . . I want
> you to fulfill these two commandments. You must
> walk, in fact, with both feet, not one, and with
> two wings fly to heaven.

This text is a perfect description of the Order's life—contemplative and apostolic. In this instruction to St. Catherine, Christ shows the friar that if he pursues his apostolic
work in the right spirit it will not separate him from God.

The Dominican apostle imitates both Christ and St.
Dominic. Both were contemplatives. Jesus spent thirty-

three years on earth; thirty were devoted to his hidden life, three to his public life. St. Dominic lived about fifty years; approximately the first ten years of his priesthood were devoted to contemplative prayer, the last sixteen to the apostolate. These facts and figures teach a great lesson: the contemplative life must precede the active life, not necessarily in time but always in importance. Contemplation is more important than action as it is the source of action.

Dominic's contemplation made him apostolic. Jordan of Saxony speaking of the Founder's years at Osma, describes his singular gift of compassionating sinners, the wretched, and the afflicted:

> Spending the nights in prayer, he was accustomed to pray to his Father most constantly behind closed doors. Occasionally during his prayers, from the groanings of his heart, he would let slip cries and words; nor was he able to contain himself, so that bursting forth he could be clearly heard from a distance. It was his frequent and special prayer to God to deign to grant him charity that was efficacious in caring for and working for the salvation of men. He considered that he himself would only then become truly a member of Christ, when he would have spent himself wholly, to the extent of his powers, in gaining souls; like the Lord Jesus, the Savior of all, who gave Himself totally for our salvation.

He prayed thus for zeal, an essential requisite for the apostle; when God answered his prayer, calling him into the apostolic field, he was ready.

Dominic found his new vocation his first night in Toulouse when he met the Albigensian innkeeper. Moved with compassion for this lost sheep, he spent the night persuading him of his errors. His years of prayer at Osma bore their first fruit as the morning dawned, when he gained the man's conversion. This conversion was a turning point for Dominic too. His craving for souls could no longer be satisfied. All the remaining years of

his life he spent seeking them. Pons, Cistercian Abbot
of Boulbonne, spoke of this zeal during the canonization
process at Toulouse: "He thirsted for souls and was fervent in prayer and preaching. The sins of men crucified
him and it could be said of him what was said of Paul
the apostle, 'Who is weak and I am not weak'" (II Cor.
11:29).

The friars who lived in close association with the
Founder emphasized this zeal.

> He had a burning zeal for the salvation of souls,
> not only of Christians, but also of Saracens and
> infidels, and he exhorted the brethren to be like-
> minded. Dominic's love for souls was so great
> that he wanted to preach to the pagans and, if
> necessary, give his life for the faith. He planned
> to do this as soon as the Order was well estab-
> lished.

John of Spain testified that Dominic ". . . preached constantly and, in every way possible, exhorted the brethren
to do the same. Sending them to preach he begged and
admonished them to be eager for the salvation of souls."

St. Catherine of Siena's zeal matched that of St.
Dominic. Raymond of Capua relates how her love for
souls developed. At the age of seven, after she had made
the vow of virginity, Catherine began to long for souls
and had an especially strong love for saints who had
labored for their salvation. About this time she discovered
that the Order of Preachers had been founded out of
zeal for the faith and the good of souls. From then on
she conceived such a high idea of this Order that whenever she saw any of the preaching friars going past her
house, she would watch where they had put their feet
and, when they had passed by, go and kiss their foot-
prints in a spirit of great humility and devotion. An
unquenchable longing to become a member of the Order
and join in its work of helping souls arose within her.

How did St. Dominic become an apostle? By keeping the *Rule of St. Augustine* and the Constitutions of the

Canons of Osma. The *Rule of St. Augustine,* patterned on the life of the apostles, powerfully develops the apostolic spirit in those who keep it. The community life prescribed by Augustine wonderfully prepares the soul to work for souls. When Gregory IX was ready to declare St. Dominic a saint, he told the priests who had come to petition for the canonization: "In Dominic I knew a man who lived the rule of the apostles in its totality." Yearning for souls and burning with zeal, he does not surprise us by founding an order of preachers whose special duty was preaching for the salvation of souls.

Expansion of the Order's Apostolate

If this is the purpose of the Order of Preachers, how can Dominicans justify the multiple ramifications and developments of the original apostolate? How can they arrive at the heart of what the Founder did? He established an apostolic Order to continue the work of Christ who came to save souls, died for them, and sent the Apostles to prolong his mission. Their primary duty was to preach: "Go into the whole world and preach the Gospel to every creature. He who believes and is baptized shall be saved, but he who does not believe shall be condemned" (Mark, 16:15-16). Their chief work was to propagate the faith and save souls.

Preaching is proclaiming the faith. We can do this in a classroom as well as in a pulpit; we can preach by good example as well as by broadcasts and books. Every action which teaches truth, which reveals the person of Christ in one way or another, can be considered the work of a Dominican. Father Vincent McNabb was so impregnated with this truth that he wanted even his corpse to preach. Calling for a plain funeral, he said:

> I don't want a shaped and polished coffin such as they usually provide, nor should I like to have a brass factory-made cross on it nor be labelled with a brass label. I want an ordinary box made of the same sort of wood as this floor.

A large cross and an inscription in black should be painted on its lid. His body should be hauled to the cemetery on a builder's truck with coffin, acolytes, and cross bearer sitting in plain view. When Fr. McNabb had completed these instructions, he continued:

> Of course, I know what some people will say: "That's McNabb and his tomfoolery, McNabb and his publicity, showing off." But it isn't that, my dear Father, it isn't that. All my life I have preached and when I am no longer alive I shall still preach. I shall preach even with my dead body. . . .

The Constitutions have long recognized that preaching could be interpreted in a wide sense. Since 1505 the successive editions have always bracketed preaching and teaching: ". . . it should be our chief concern to be useful to the souls of our neighbor. With this particular end is closely connected teaching and defending the truths of the Catholic Church both by word in the schools and by different kinds of teaching." Should St. Dominic, who used all the avenues that were open to him to spread the faith, return today, he most certainly would urge his children to enter the educational field and use audio-visual and the many other new methods of reaching souls.

He would even be pleased with the singing apostolate of Sister Sourire, whose recordings bring "light music with a message." Her collection of gentle folk songs (she is composer, lyricist, and soloist) poignantly demonstrate that the things of God are gay, not gloomy; that no earthly thing is alien to his service. Her "Dominique" is the most popular of all her songs:

> Dominic, Oh Dominic,
>   Over the land he plods along
> And sings a little song,
>   Never looking for reward
> He just talks about the Lord

To bring back the straying liars
And the lost sheep to the fold,
He brought forth the Preaching Friars,
Heaven's soldiers, brave and bold.

Grant us now, Oh Dominic,
The grace of love and simple mirth,
That we all may help to quicken,
Godly love and trust on earth.

When told that her album had become an international best-seller, the Singing Sister replied:

I'm glad, because it carries a message to the world outside our walls. In Fichermont our religious life is not as strict and stifling as people think. We laugh, we smile, we sing, and I guess my songs prove that.

Although St. Dominic dealt with the conditions of the early thirteenth century and could not have foreseen how his Order would deveolp, he did not want it to stagnate. His own spirit was progressive. He did not scruple to make innovations to meet the problems of his time. The whole concept of his Order with its worldwide preaching mission and many of its means, such as the use made of the powers of dispensation, the abandonment of manual labor, the strong reliance on doctrine and study, the adoption of strict poverty, the development of a centralized, yet democratic, government, were new. Dominic's spirit was as broad and Catholic as that of the Church.

This Catholic quality and the Christlike character of the Founder were impressively illustrated in a vision accorded to St. Catherine of Siena. God the Father himself compared Dominic to Christ and Dominicans to the Apostles:

The holy Virgin asserted that she saw in a vision the Supreme and Eternal Father producing from His mouth, His co-eternal Son, who was clearly

shown to her in the human nature which he had
assumed. And while she was contemplating him,
she saw the Blessed Patriarch Dominic come
forth from the breast of the Father, surrounded
with light and splendor, and she heard a voice
come forth from the same mouth, saying: "Beloved daughter, I have begotten these two sons—
one by nature, the other by sweet and tender
adoption." Now as Catherine stood amazed at
this comparison so elevated, which rendered
equal, so to speak, a saint with Jesus Christ, he
who had uttered these surprizing words explained
them himself.

. . . Just as this My natural Son, as eternal word
of my mouth, spoke openly to the world whatever
I charged him to say, and bore witness
to the truth, as he himself said to Pilate, so too
my son by adoption, Dominic, preached openly
to the world the truth of my words, both among
heretics and among Catholics, and not only while
he lived, but also through his successors, through
whom he still preaches and will always preach.
For just as my Son by nature sent His disciples,
so my son by adoption sent his friars.

The comparison of our holy father with Christ need
not stop at this point; we can carry it further. When Our
Lord died, the Church was in its infancy but he had
given it all.it needed to grow. The Apostles had received
their preaching mission. Today the Catholic apostolate
has evolved in thousands of ways. Never did the Apostles
realize all the things the Catholic Church would be doing
in the twentieth century. Yet no one asks whether these
activities are a legitimate development of what Our Lord
intended, despite the fact that preaching was the primary
commission given to the Apostles. If the pope and bishops
approve an activity, we know that it is Catholic and
apostolic.

In 1221, when its Founder died, the Order of Friars
Preachers was an infant Order; it had three monasteries

of nuns, perhaps twenty-five priories, and about 250 friars. But in founding it, Dominic had given it all it needed to grow. Above all, he had given his sons their preaching mandate. Today, contemplating the Order, we see that this mission has unfolded in hundreds of ways. We do not question whether this is legitimate. Rather, we look back through the pages of history and witness how the Order, guided by the masters general and the general chapters, adapted its apostolate, bringing it up-to-date in each new age according to the principles laid down by St. Dominic. This constant "aggiornamento" continues under the same enlightened guidance.

Let us examine a case to see how the early friars interpreted the mind of their Founder. In 1217 he sent eight of his disciples to study at the University of Paris. Less than ten years after his death, when the opportunity came to take a chair of theology at the University, the friars took it, becoming professors even though St. Dominic probably never considered this possible. Actually the University itself was developing. In 1221 no one could have predicted the tremendous intellectual changes that would take place there. Dominic's sons, especially under the leadership of Jordan of Saxony, Dominic's successor, Humbert of Romans, Albert, and Thomas, carried the Order into the heart of this expanding academic universe. This evolution was a natural growth from the seed the Founder planted in 1217.

During the Master-generalship of Jordan, while many of Dominic's earliest disciples were still living, the Order took on the following works: university teaching, foreign missions, and the Inquisition. Dominicans were soon solving social problems, reforming monasteries, visiting dioceses for the pope, helping to found other Orders, serving as confessors to kings and advisors to bishops. They were aiding people to make wills, acting as ambassadors and arbitrators. Though the Order regretted seeing so many friars engage in work of this kind, because it feared that preaching would fade into the background, it did not stop them. If Jordan of Saxony or the first disciples had thought that these activities were against the will of their holy father, they would have had to protest and forbid them. On the contrary, when new ways of saving souls opened to the friars, who did not interpret preaching in the narrow sense, they entered them.

The Order's Flexibility

Such expansion of the Order's works was possible because the Founder had made his Order apostolic, giving it the adaptability that enabled it at all times to achieve its end—the salvaion of souls through preaching. He attained this effect by embodying the power of dispensation in the Constitutions, authorizing the prior to dispense from monastic observances when any of them stood in the way of "preaching, study, or the salvation of souls." The eminent Franciscan historian, Archbishop Paschal Robinson, stressed the importance of the power of dispensation in an address he delivered in 1916, during the seventh centenary celebration of the Order of Friars Preachers:

> I would point out another novel feature which stands out in Dominic's rule and which is quite peculiar to his Order, namely: the principle of dispensation. At the head of the Constitutions the principle of dispensation appears jointly with the very definition of the Order's purpose, and is placed before the text of the laws to show that it controls and tempers their application—a thing quite unknown under that form in the older religious rules. This system of dispensation, properly understood, may be called truly the masterpiece of Dominican legislation. It has, in a great degree, enabled the Order to bend itself to new needs and to preserve its unity. It is also a perfect instrument of the ascertic spirit, entailing, as it does, a surrender at all times of small views and low aims.

A Dominican, therefore, is never scandalized when superiors grant dispensations. They are not intended primarily for the good of the friar (except when he is sick or incapacitated) but for the good of the apostolate. When given for that purpose they do not weaken the religious spirit, for they are then unselfish and motivated by zeal.

The history of the Order in the United States proves that Dominicans in the New World understood the spirit of their Founder. When the welfare of souls called, they were quick to enter new fields of labor. Father Edward Dominic Fenwick, an American member of the English province, brought the Order to the United States with the cherished hope of establishing a college in Maryland. Priests were badly needed everywhere in the new Republic, and he hoped that his school would be a nursery of many vocations. But Bishop John Carroll pointed across the Allegheny Mountains to the missionary fields. Thus a century-long struggle began on the frontier. Vocations were few and the hardships great. The priests of the province covered the old Midwest and Northwest on horseback with their Mass kits in their saddle bags to keep faith alive among the scattered Catholic settlements. Fenwick himself became the Apostle of Ohio. The tremendous increase of vocations and development of activities after 1900 may be a divine reward for the labor and sacrifice of the early fathers.

The toil of the frontier did not mark the limit of the province's sacrifices. Fr. Bernard Walker describes vividly the Order's contributions to the Church in the United States.

> During the sixty years (1807-1867) the Province of St. Joseph was developing, . . . the total number of those who entered the Order in America, and made profession, was less than one hundred; . . . So hard was the life that eight students died before ordination; twelve who attained the priesthood survived less than five or six years on the

missions; and ten more gave their lives ministering to the plague-sticken in one or other of the epidemics so frightening and fatal in those days. There were never more than forty priests at any one time in the Province. . . And yet six of those early brethren were chosen for the episcopacy before the Civil War . . . Only one other religious institute in America gave so many of its subjects to the hierarchy in the period under discussion. It may truly be said that the interests and development of the Order were sacrificed for the good of the Church in our country for nearly a century.

When the pioneering period of St. Joseph's Province closed with the end of the Civil War, preaching became the dominant activity of the fathers, especially in conducting parochial missions, a work that brought them to the great cities, and back to the Atlantic seaboard. Their mission bands were unmatched in this apostolate, so reminiscent of the age of St. Dominic. Men like Fathers Charles Hyacinth McKenna, Clement Thuente, and Ignatius Smith drew overflowing crowds into the churches when they entered the pulpits.

Father Walter Farrell, in a sense, began a new era. Primarily a teacher, he labored most of his priestly life in the houses of study, but alongside this academic work he developed a busy career as writer, lecturer, retreat master, confessor, and director of souls. He is best known for his four-volume work, *A Companion to the Summa,* an eminently successful adaptation of the *Summa Theologiae* of St. Thomas to the modern age. Father James M. Gillis, C.S.P., himself a great preacher and journalist, expressed his pleasure in discovering

> . . . in what is at once a translation and a running commentary of the *Summa,* wit and humor and epigrammatic expression. They are there . . . wit, wisdom, humor. And the marvel of it is that as the author says (he is an author though he might call himself only a translator and ex-

positor) "the whole work is not a book about the *Summa*" but the *Summa* itself reduced to popular language.

The career of Fr. Farrell perhaps exemplifies the many accommodations American Dominicans have made to modern needs. Beginning with their pioneering days, moving through the stage of parochial missions, entering into the foreign mission fields in China, Pakistan, Nigeria, Chile, Peru, and Bolivia, and terminating in the educational and Newman Club work of the current period, the fathers have attempted to keep abreast of the changing scene.

Dominican sisters have joined them in making these adaptations. Father Thomas Wilson, prior of St. Rose, Kentucky, knew how to evoke a spirit of sacrifice in young Catholic women. He appealed to his congregation in February, 1822, for vocations to the sisterhood. Katherine Burton describes the result:

> He was not prepared for what followed his plea. He had hoped that two or three would answer his appeal for he had noted that several of the young women present were listening intently. He was not prepared to have eight volunteers.

Together with Angela Sansbury, one of the volunteers, Father Wilson founded the first congregation of Dominican sisters in the United States. Mother Angela also founded a second motherhouse in Ohio. The Kentucky experience was duplicated by Father Samuel Mazuchelli, who established a community in Wisconsin. In 1853 the American sisters were joined by a heroic band of volunteer Second Order nuns who came from Regensburg, Germany, to aid in the work of education. A dozen Third Order congregations have sprung from the foundation they made in Brooklyn. Domincan sisters stood, indeed, in the vanguard of the American Catholic educational apostolate. Most of the thirty motherhouses devote themselves to education.

Dominican sensitiveness to current needs continued to be manifested. Mother Alphonsa (Rose Hawthorne Lathrop, daughter of Nathaniel Hawthorne) and Mother Mary Walsh entered the apostolate of mercy. Describing the aims of the Dominican Servants of Relief for Incurable Cancer she had founded, Mother Rose wrote:

> I am trying to serve the poor as a servant. I wish to serve the cancerous poor because they are avoided more than any other class of sufferers; and I wish to go to them as a poor creature myself, though powerful to help through the open-handed gifts of public kindness, because it is by humility and sacrifice that we become worthy to feel the holy spirit of pity and to carry into the disorders of destitute sickness the cheerful love we have gathered from the Heavenly Kingdom for distribution.

Mother Mary Walsh established the Dominican Sisters of the Sick Poor. They pursue a home missionary apostolate centered in nursing the sick poor in their own homes regardless of race, color, or creed. Both communities find many opportunities of ministering not only to the physical but also to the spiritual needs of the poor.

The Maryknoll Sisters were the first to carry American Dominicans into the foreign mission field. The Dominican Mission Sisters, founded in Chicago in 1953, have chosen catechetical and social work in the United States and foreign missions all over the world as their apostolate. Their first missionary bands have gone to the understaffed missions of Latin America.

These examples are impressive proof that Dominican Sisters share in the apostolic mission of their Order. Every religious, indeed, by the very fact of taking vows becomes an apostle in spirit, desiring the salvation of all men. As His Excellency Archbishop Paul Phillipe, O.P., writes in his *The Ends of the Religious Life according to St. Thomas Aquinas*:

> . . . Christian perfection comprises contempla-
> tion of God and love of neighbor; one cannot
> really love God, if one does not seek to know
> him and if one does not love his neighbor. Every
> religious, even the most active, must tend to and
> may attain the perfection of contemplation—the
> lives of the saints offer us many examples of great
> contemplatives in the active life. Likewise, every
> religious, even though exclusively contemplative
> and solitary, must desire the salvation of all men
> and can collaborate in it through his prayer
> and penitential life. In other words, contemplation
> and love of neighbor are part of the general end
> of every religious Institute, because they are
> elements of Christian perfection . . .

If this is true of members of every religious Order and Congregation, it is especially true of Dominicans. They belong to the Order of Preachers, an institute entrusted by the Church with the mission to preach, the supreme apostolic function. We can illustrate how its members contribute to this work by looking at the life of the laybrothers. They do not enter the pulpit, the classroom, or the ministry, yet they are apostolic because they are integral members of the Order of Preachers. By vow they belong to it and share its work. The brothers free the priests for study, prayer, and preaching by relieving them of many duties. They help with their own very efficacious prayers and sacrifices. It is said that when Lacordaire preached his famed sermons in the pulpit of Notre Dame, a brother sat beneath the pulpit praying his rosary. Perhaps in the eyes of God the brothers' rosary did more good than the preacher's words. This is all implicit in the official name given the brothers as recently as 1958 by the general chapter of Caleruega. No longer are they to be known as laybrothers but as brother cooperators. This is what they have always been, but now are so in name as well.

Contemplative nuns, also, do not engage directly in

the apostolate but by vow are incorporated into apostolic Order. They "strive after Christian perfection; and by means of that perfection, implore for the labors of their brethren abundant fruits in holiness." By their prayers and sacrificial lives they implore grace for their brothers and sisters working directly for souls.

Sisters of the Third Order and tertiaries also participate in the Order's apostolate, helping by their prayers, sacrifices, and holy lives. In addition, the sisters actually teach Catholic truth. It is not necessary to stand in the pulpit to do that. Most priests spend far more time speaking to one soul in a confessional or parlor than they do preaching in the pulpit. A nursing sister may teach truth to a sick person in a hospital ward.

Sisters as members of the laity, may not teach as bishops and priests do; nevertheless, schools and hospitals are places where the truth may be proclaimed. Furthermore, Dominican sisters, as members of a congregation ecclesiastically approved and incorporated into the Dominican family, are invested by the Church with a mission that carries with it a command and an office to teach. They fulfill a definite role, one that is official, juridical, and canonical. They collaborate with the hierarchy in carrying out its work of sanctification and government, not because they have the sacred powers of orders and jurisdiction, but because their Congregation is definitely commissioned to instruct the faithful in Christian doctrine. This teaching is primarily the pastor's office, but sisters, as members of an approved religious family, have a mandate to aid him.

In his *Summa Theologiae,* St. Thomas discusses the special graces of which St. Paul speaks in his first Epistle to the Corinthians, such as the grace of working miracles or prophesying (*Summa theol.,* II—II, q. 177). Among these Paul classes the grace of the word (*gratia sermonis, et sapientiae, et scientiae*) (I Cor. 12:8). This is a preeminent grace given sometimes to the preacher, teacher, or writer, not for his own spiritual benefit but so that he may more effectively instruct those who listen to him, that he may move them to hear the word of God eagerly and with joy and that he may induce them to love his doctrine and carry it out. Women also, Thomas writes, even though they do not teach as bishops and priests do, may receive this grace when they teach the word of God; for example, a mother instructing her children or a sister exercising her spiritual motherhood in the classroom. But God does not always give this special apostolic grace. Why he does in some cases and not in others is a mystery. It cannot be merited. It is only possible for the preacher or his hearers to remove the obstacles to its bestowal by their prayers or good works. Moreover, once given, it may be lost in two ways: either through the fault of the speaker who seeks for glory or applause, or through the sin of the hearers who in some way resist it.

Even when it is not a question of this special grace, both the speaker and his audience must rely on ordinary grace: the speaker to prepare and carry out his assignment, the hearer to receive God's word with fruit. It is one thing to proclaim the word; another to preach with spiritual fruit. It is grace which causes the words of the preacher, teacher, or writer to fructify in the souls of those whom he reaches. That is why we give so much credit to Lacordaire's laybrother. His prayers begged graces for both preacher and audience. "Unless the Holy Spirit fills the hearts of the listeners," wrote St. Gregory the Great, "in vain does the voice of the teacher resound in their ears."

The personal life of the apostle, therefore, is intimately connected with his apostolic work. Since he must rely on grace if he wants to produce fruit worthy of heaven, he must fear to place obstacles in the way of grace, fear to impede God's generosity by a life that is lukewarm or poorly motivated. He must so live as to receive grace; he should pray for it and hope for it. He may even hope to receive, if God so wills, the grace of the word.

At this point we again contact the genius of the Dominican Order. The Dominican contemplates, hoping that when he has gazed on the truths of faith and his heart has been fired with love for God, he may carry his knowledge and love to his hearers. It is this inner life which makes his apostolic life germinate. When priests preach and sisters teach, they hope that their words, pregnant with grace, will bear fruit, that their audience will hearken to the word of God and obey it.

Sanctity Needed for the Apostolate

To be a true apostle, then, a Dominican must sanctify himself first. In all his endeavors, he must go back constantly to that starting-point, his own sanctification. "An apostolic message that has not been shaped in the sanctuary, in the choir, and in the cloister is never complete." The Constitutions stress personal sanctification at their very outset:

> As the Rule admonishes us, the first reason why
> we are gathered together is that we might dwell
> together in harmony in the house, and there may
> be in us but one mind and one heart in God,
> so that we may be found perfect in charity.

The road to personal holiness is the first thing that the Constitutions instruct the master of novices to teach his subjects:

> Before everything else, let the master of novices
> teach them and assiduously recommend to them
> that they totally fulfill the precept about the
> love of God and neighbor whcih stands at the
> head of the Rule . . . .

The Constitutions of the Second Order also emphasize personal holiness: "The Nuns of the Sacred Order of Preachers . . . strive after Christian perfection." It is only then that their apostolic work is mentioned: ". . . and by means of that perfection, implore for the labors of their

brethren abundant fruit in holiness." The Constitutions of
the Third Order are even more explicit:

> The Order of our holy father St. Dominic was
> instituted for the sanctification of its members
> and the salvation of souls. The principal and
> essential end of our congregation is, then, the
> personal sanctification of the sisters.

Their Constitutions immediately link this primary aim to
the apostolate. "The secondary or special end is the education of Catholic youth, care of orphans, the nursing of the
sick, or the conducting of retreat houses." Personal holiness is the source of the apostolate. A saintly life clears
away the obstacles obstructing the graces needed for working among souls.

The means St. Dominic gave his children to make
them apostles are identical with those that make them
holy. This was to be expected for the two ends are but
one. The charity which leads the Dominican to seek
union with God, prompts him to love his neighbor and
work for his salvation. The means established by our holy
Founder are, first, the vows of religion and the community
life. Then come the liturgy, other prayers, monastic observances: fasts, abstinence, silence, and all the practices
which Rule, Constitutions, and custom impose. These
means fill their double purpose, sanctifying the member
and preparing for the apostolate. Prayers implore God's
mercy, make reparation, and beg graces for sinners. When
the Dominican steps from the sanctuary, choir, or cloister
into the ministry, he has already prepared the way.

The means established by the Order enable the friar
to help souls by living a sacrificial life. He imitates St.
Dominic who offered himself through his vows as a holocaust, giving himself to be consumed completely in the
Divine service. He continued to sacrifice himself daily
by utmost fidelity to the observances of his religious life.
After he became an apostle, he prized the observances

not only for their sacrificial quality but also for their apostolic value. During his entire life as a preacher, he did his utmost to carry the recollection of the cloister with him, fulfilling as far as possible the monastic duties of his state, keeping the silence, reciting the canonical hours at the prescribed times, praying long into the night after his preaching day was done.

But even though the Order's contemplative and apostolic lives are so well integrated, it is difficult under the hectic conditions of the twentieth century to carry the spirit of contemplation into the apostolate. Dominican sisters especially are making exceptional sacrifices to bear their heavy load of teaching. They give a considerable part of their day to classes, cutting deeply into their time for the community and prayer. They teach all day, have meetings, debates, plays. Then they come back to their convent and begin preparations for the next day. If only the load could be lightened — fewer classes, fewer extraneous activities, so there would not be so much rushing, so little time for silence and solitude.

St. Catherine of Siena, the special patroness of Dominican sisters, has taught them how to overcome this difficulty and preserve their recollection. When her family deprived her of her room and made her "do all the menial work in the kitchen," they took away both the time and place for prayer and meditation. Raymond of Capua relates how she solved her problem:

> Under the inspiration of the Holy Spirit she began to build up in her mind a secret cell which she vowed she would never leave for anything in the world . . .having made herself an inner cell which no one could take from her, she had no need ever to come out of it again . . . Catherine built for herself a cell not made with human hands, helped inwardly by Christ, and so was untroubled about losing a room made with walls

built by men. I remember [Raymond continues] that whenever I used to find myself pressed with too much business, or had to go on a journey, Catherine would say again and again, "Make yourself a cell in your own mind from which you need never come out."

Father Gerald Vann in his own inimitable way made a modern version of this same advice:

> . . . to be contemplative means to be a prayerful person, and that means to be a person who is thoughtful before God. Now, this does not necessitate a great deal of *physical* stillness. Many saints have led lives of intense activity; and Brother Lawrence, the 17th-century Carmelite laybrother, describes how he learned to live quietly and continuously with God amidst the clatter of his kitchen.

To animate themselves for their apostolic burden, Dominicans should reflect that St. Dominic had to sacrifice the peace and quiet of his cloister for years of constant traveling and preaching. The real preacher would remain in the priory or the convent adoring God if his neighbor did not need him. Adoration is better than preaching or teaching, but the Dominican loves God so ardently that he leaves his community and goes out to preach and teach for the salvation of souls. St. Thomas describes his apostolic spirit:

> There are some who have ascended to such a summit of charity that they even put aside divine contemplation, though they delight greatly in it, that they may serve God through the salvation of their neighbors; and this perfection appears in Paul (see Rom. 9:3 and Phil. 1:23). Such also is the perfection proper to prelates and preachers and whosoever works to bring about the salvation of others. Hence they are symbolized by the angels on the ladder of Jacob, ascending through contemplation, descending, however, through the

solicitude they feel for the salvation of their
neighbors (*De carit.*, a. 11, ad 6).

This is what the Dominican sister does daily when she
enters the classroom. "Laying aside for the love of God
the sweetness of the contemplative life, which she per-
fers, she takes up the occupations of the active life to
obtain the salvation of her neighbors" (St. Thomas,
Quodl. I, q. 7, a. 14, ad 2). This sacrifice is pleasing in
God's eyes, motivated as it is by love and obedience.
She goes into the classroom to reveal the person of Christ
to teach her pupils to know and love him. He is with her
when she goes to the classroom in this spirit. As she rises
from her contemplation, Christ says to her as he said to
St. Catherine of Siena: "I have no intention of cutting
you off from me. On the contrary, I wish to bind you
more closely to myself by means of love of neighbor. . . ."

A natural mother gives birth to her child in pain and
sacrifice. The religious sister experiences the pain of many
hours of separation from her Eucharistic Lord. She feels
the sacrifice she makes of her prayer life to make possible
her work in the classroom. Are not these the pain and
sacrifice of spiritual maternity? This sounds idealistic but
is factual and real. There is a spiritual maternity. Who
else but the sisters, under God, are doing so much for souls
in the United States? Priests do something far greater
in administering the Sacraments and saying Mass, but
the cost is far less to them personally. The Mass and the
Sacraments come from God. Contemplative nuns with
their rigorous austerities and strictly cloistered lives are
not called upon to make the contribution of nervous
energy, to experience the constant tension, to make such
unceasing efforts to remain recollected. The pangs of
spiritual maternity are a reality.

The members of the Order love their vocation. Living it, they imitate both the hidden and public lives of
Christ and St. Dominic. They prove effectively that they
love God. "As long as you did it for one of these, the

least of my brethren," Our Lord said, "you did it for me" (Matt., 25:40). When the Dominican serves his neighbor, wherever it may be, he is serving Christ. He fulfills the two great commandments of the law, the love of God and the love of neighbor. He remains faithful to his own Rule: "Before all things, dear brethren, love God and then your neighbor, for these are the chief precepts which have been given to us."

ST. DOMINIC IN CHOIR

Chapter V

DOMINICAN LIFE

is

LITURGICAL

We have examined the ends of the Order—contemplation and the apostolate, the first frutifying in the second. These are the noble goals that the Order sets before the Dominican. However, it is not enough to have marvelous ideals. It is necessary to have suitable means to achieve them. St. Dominic endowed the Order with powerful means perfectly adapted to the ideals he envisioned. The Constitutions of the First Order precisely summarize the most important of these means:

> The means set by our most holy Patriarch for the attainment of our end are, besides the three solemn vows of obedience, chasity, and poverty, the regular life with its monastic observances, the solemn chanting of the Divine Office and assiduous study of sacred truth. With us these things cannot be taken away or substantially changed, although, with the exception of the vows, they may be opportunely tempered, according to the circumstances of time and place, so that they be made more suited for the attainment of the end and be imparted a greater efficacy.

The Constitutions of the nuns use almost the same language to describe the chief means to achieve perfection.

> The means given to the nuns by the holy Patriarch Saint Dominic, for the attainment of this end [perfection], and transmitted to us by venerable tradition, are especially: the three solemn vows of poverty, chastity, and obedience; the solemn recitation of the Divine Office; certain fasts and bodily mortifications; and the devout and constant contemplation of Our Lord, Creator, Redeemer, and Sanctifier.

The Constitutions of the Third Order Sisters, in slightly different form, prescribe similar means. The sisters take the religious vows; chant in choir the Office of the Blessed Mother (some of them chant the Divine Office); have their hours of mental prayer; live the comunity life—common table, nourishment, furniture, clothing; keep the monastic observances—silence, fasts, abstinence, chapter of faults; and wear the Dominican habit and contemplative scapular.

Tertiaries follow a rule which, in accord with their life in the world, parallels that of the fathers and sisters. They promise to live according to the Order's spirit, attend Mass every day, if possible, and recite either the Office of the Blessed Mother or the fifteen mysteries of the rosary. They hold their monthly chapter meeting and endeavor to achieve a deeper understanding of the truths of the faith. In all branches of the Dominican family the same goals are pursued, fundamentally the same means are employed, and the same spirit is engendered and maintained. In this chapter we shall discuss only the prayer life of the Dominican.

Dominican Contemplative Life and the Liturgy

In seeking to make its children contemplative apostles, the Order demands of them, as an indispensable condition, a life of prayer. It frames their daily life in prayer, prescribing that they carry out the liturgy and fulfill many other spiritual obligations. Furthermore, it creates an atmosphere of prayer in its houses, enjoining silence as the essential environment in which Dominicans shall lead their lives.

The Dominican day gravitates around the liturgy. The supreme act of the day is the sacrifice of the Mass, the highest praise man can offer to the Holy Trinity. Providing a setting for the Mass is the Divine Office. It prepares for the Mass and draws from it, carrying its graces into the entire day. Distributed at key points in the daily schedule, the Office consecrates every part of the day to the divine service, sanctifying each passing hour with some liturgical act.

Only as a consequence of his primary commitment to the service of God and the sanctification of his own soul, does the Dominican leave the cloister and work for the salvation of his neighbor. The Rule of St. Augustine, read repeatedly in the Order's refectories, impresses this truth upon him: "Before all things, beloved brethren, love God and then your neighbor."

In his supreme work as a man of prayer, the Dominican resembles the Incarnate Word, the Second Person of the Blessed Trinity made Man. Christ is both God and Man. As man he stands at the head of the whole human race and is the supreme Adorer of the heavenly Father. As man, he gives infinite praise to the Trinity, because he is a Divine Person. He has the nature of God and the nature of man. The Person acting in these two natures is Divine. Since a person's actions are measured by his dignity, Our Lord's acts, even those he performs in his human nature, are of infinite value. When Christ, as man, adores the heavenly Father, his worship is infinite. Acting thus, he fulfills the first obligation of every man, that is, he adores the heavenly Father. The friar, participating in the liturgy, continues the adoration which Christ the Lord performed on earth.

The obligation to adore also falls upon the Dominican

as a religious. On entering the Order, he consecrates himself by vow to God's service. From that day forth it is his duty to join in the corporate praise which his Order offers uninterruptedly before the throne of God.

Through its solemn worship, the Order of Preachers imitates our Holy Mother the Church, God's society on earth, which exists to praise and adore the Supreme Being. Within the Church, the Order constitutes a special group of adorers. Each of its parts is united to the others by the supernatural bonds of profession for the holy purpose of praising God. Furthermore, all its branches work together as a family to multiply, by their apostolic works, adorers of the Trinity. To achieve this end most effectively, the Order seeks to make its members contemplatives, living images of Christ, the perfect Adorer.

The Heritage of St. Dominic

Love for the liturgy is a precious heritage Dominicans owe to their Founder. He himself was completely committed to the liturgy—a commitment we find expressed in his life, in the Constitutions, and in the way he taught his children.

By profession he was a cannon regular. He was a priest whose chief duty was to carry out the sacred liturgy in the cathedral of Osma. His life centered around the Divine Office, for he was obliged as a duty of his state to participate daily in chanting the canonical hours. His spirituality, therefore, was basically a priestly spirituality.

The Mass was his life. He was so moved during the sacred mysteries that he wept when reciting the Canon of the Mass and the *Pater Noster*. This weeping reveals the mystic who almost sees beyond the veil of the Sacrament. Mystically, Dominic sees Christ present on the altar, the Lamb slain and still bearing His wounds. The testimony of Stephen of Spain describes the devotion of Dominic at Mass.

The witness very frequently saw him celebrate Mass and always noticed that his eyes and cheeks were wet with tears during the Canon. It was quite easy for those present to perceive his devotion, his great fervor during Mass, and the way he said the *Pater Noster.* The witness never remembers having seen him say Mass with dry eyes.

Frogier of Penna had also observed the same devotion: "I saw the Blessed Dominic say Mass many times both in the monastery and on journeys. And there was not a single time when Dominic did not shed tears." The meaning of the sacred mysteries overpowered him.

Even after he became an apostle, St. Dominic continued his liturgical life. Though he frequently went on journeys lasting days and weeks, he celebrated Mass each day he was near a church. He demonstrated that it is possible to be both contemplative and apostolic. Saying Mass every day does not sound heroic to priests of the twentieth century. Now priests say daily Mass, but it was not so in the thirteenth century. This explains why so many medieval biographers stress that their saint said Mass daily. We find this in the lives of St. Dominic, St. Thomas, and St. Vincent Ferrer. Such devotion to the Mass was especially remarkable in the lives of itinerant apostles like Dominic and Vincent. Vincent carried with him a company of friars who chanted the Office with him and became his choir when he sang the daily High Mass. Paul of Venice testified that Dominic also loved to sing the Mass. "Even while traveling, he was devout and constant in prayer. If he could find a suitable church, he went to celebrate High Mass every day." These words tell us much about Dominic's way of preaching. He preached so constantly, moving about and preaching everywhere, that often the day's end found him far from a church. He then stopped at an inn or wrapped his cappa around himself and rested by the roadside. "When he came to an inn," remarked Ventura of Verona, "if there was a church there, he always went to pray in the church. Even traveling, he celebrated Mass almost every day, if he found a church."

St. Dominic's Love for the Divine Office

Dominic's love for the liturgy included not only the Mass but the Divine Office. He taught the early friars to chant the canonical hours at the prescribed time, if possible, even when they were en route. Ventura again supplies our information:

> Almost always when outside the priory, on hearing the first stroke of the matins bell from the monasteries, he used to arise and arouse the friars; with great devotion he celebrated the whole night and day Office at the prescribed hours so that he omitted nothing. And after compline, when traveling, he kept and had his companions keep silence, just as though they were in the priory.

It was the same when he was at home in the priory. "Devoted to the Divine Office," Rudolph of Faenza tells us, "the Blessed Dominic always attended choir with the community." He did this even when he had stayed up all night praying. There is striking proof of his fidelity to choir from his last week on earth. During the greater part of July, 1221, Dominic had worked in Lombardy, preaching in many cities of the area. Toward the end of the month, he came back to Bologna fatigued and running a fever. Ventura lets us see his valiant spirit:

> Because of the excessive heat, the prior suggested to Brother Dominic that he go to rest and not rise for matins during the night. The holy man did not acquiesce in this suggestion but entered the church and prayed through the night. Nevertheless, he was present at matins.

The Founder constantly exhorted the brethren to put their hearts into the Office. Paul of Venice tells us of this characteristic:

> He would walk around on each side of the choir urging the brethren by word and example to sing

well and attentively and to recite the psalms devoutly. He himself was so faithfully intent on what he was praying that he was never distracted by any tumult or noise.

Dominic was just as intent on private prayer. Even during his missionary years among the Albigensians he readily became absorbed in God. One witness tells us: "When we searched for him, we found him on his knees, despite danger from the wild wolves that infested the place." Throughout his lifetime, he passed the greater part, and frequently the whole, of the night in prayer. "We often found him in church weeping and praying," testified Ventura of Verona. "Even while traveling," said Paul of Venice. "he was devoted and constant in prayer." Few of Dominic's children have reached the degree or constancy of his prayer. But he was the Founder, and God gave him a special gift. Through his nightly prayers and vigils he won graces for the whole Order, not only for the Order as it was in his day, but for the Order as it is today and all the days of the world. His mortifications and prayers are still active for his children.

The Order's Prayer-Life

The Founder was not content to give example. He committed his Order to praise from the first moment of its existence when he had it incorporated into the family of canons regular. This was done officially by Pope Honorius III in 1216 with the bull of confirmation. For centuries thereafter the Prologue of the Constitutions contained the words: "It is fitting that we who live under one rule and vow should find union in the observances of our canonical religion." In addition the opening sections of the Constitutions regulated the celebration of conventual Mass and the recitation of the canonical hours. The present Constitutions warn, at the very outset, that the choral recitation of Divine Office is a Dominican duty which can never be radically altered.

Besides this basic Divine worship, the Order has im-

posed on its members other prayer obligations: the daily
rosary, periods of meditation, grace before and after meals,
prayers for deceased brethren and benefactors, chapter
prayers, and processions. There is a weekly *Libera* procession for the dead and processions on each of the four
Sundays of the month in honor, respectively, of Our Lady
of the Rosary, the Holy Name, the Blessed Sacrament, and
St. Dominic.

Silence—The Atmosphere of Prayer

To establish and preserve an atmosphere of prayer in
the Order's houses, St. Dominic imposed strict silence on
his children. It is to be kept throughout the priory except
in the recreation room during times of relaxation. The
primitive constitutions and those of today single out four
places for deeper silence: the dormitory (this is the resi-
dence areas), the cell, the refectory, and the choir. There
is also a solemn silence from the close of day until morning.
Even at meals, contrary to the custom of the world which
makes of meals festive occasions, Dominicans keep silence.
If they must speak for any reason, it must be in a few
words. Meals are linked to the liturgy of the choir. The
community assembles in the "cloister of the dead" waiting
to enter the refectory for meals. This particular corridor
of the cloister passage-ways is so named because in earlier
centuries the deceased were actaully buried beneath its
stones. It was there that St. Dominic wanted to be buried
"under the feet of his brethen." These considerations,
explain the deep silence of the "cloister of the dead." It
is a place of intercession for departed brothers and sisters
who can no longer do anything for themselves. As the
community enters the refectory, the brethen recite the
De profundis. Then the lengthy chant preceding the meal
begins. The grace after meals is a beautiful liturgical service which begins in the refectory and is continued as the
friars go in procession to choir where it is terminated.
Meals are taken within this liturgical framework to remind
the religious that every part of their life is dedicated to

the glorification of God. Even eating is a duty symbolizing the more sacred duty of nourishing the soul on Divine truth. "Not by bread alone does man live but by every word that comes forth from the mouth of God" (Matt. 4:4 To remind the community of this truth, meals begin and end with readings from the Sacred Scriptures. During meals, the brethen listen to the book that is read to them so that (as the *Rule of St. Augustine* puts it) "not only their mouths take in food, but their ears drink in the word of God." Meals framed in a context of worship and spiritual reading assume the character of a sacramental and continue the friar's life of adoration.

The strict silence which the Order imposes is necessary and has a Dominican motivation. It not merely serves the negative purpose of mortifying the religious, but fulfills the far nobler function of creating a prayerful climate in the house. By withdrawing from the noises of the world, by silencing his tongue, and by stilling the inner turmoil of his memory and imagination the friar recollects himself and mentally kneels in adoration before Almighty God.

The Liturgy and the Apostolate

Why did St. Dominic, an apostle founding an apostolic Order, insist so strongly on the liturgy? The two things seem to be in contradiction: long hours in the choir and the whole world clamoring for preachers. In the first instance he was a contemplative founding a contemplative Order, whose first duty would be to praise God. The prayerful soul is carried away by the beauty of God and is ravished by his love. It seeks nothing more than to adore and return his love. It would like to remain forever before him. Through the liturgy, the Church on earth remains continually in prayer before the throne of God. Dominic, the contemplative, would have nothing less for his Order than this constant adoration of God.

The holy Patriarch made his Order liturgical so that his children might bear witness to the truths they preach and teach. Christ witnessed to these truths throughout his life: "This is why I was born, and why I have come into the world, to bear witness to the truth" (John, 18:37). He gave his supreme testimony on Calvary, testifying by the sacrifice of his life that God is the Lord and Master to whom we owe everything, even our lives. The Mass like the Cross is the perfect act of worship. It is the act, infinite in value, of a Divine Person. During it, we join with Christ in witnessing to the supreme excellence of God.

The Office, the natural accompaniment of the Mass, through its psalms, hymns, and antiphons prolongs the sacrifice of praise offered by Christ on the altar. With St. Paul we say: "Through Him, therefore, let us offer a sacrifice of praise always to God, that is, the fruit of lips praising his name" (Heb. 13:15).

Through Mass and Office, Dominicans penetrate the truths of faith, nourish their souls on them and prepare to preach them. Fervent preaching springs from fervent praying. Singing God's glory in the liturgy, the friars become apostles because its texts teach them how sinners have strayed from God, violating his rights. It instills in them a longing to make reparation, to go forth and evangelize the souls redeemed by Christ. Fired by the liturgy, the friar apostle is willing to leave for a time the delights of contemplation to preach the word. Very aptly, the Order has taken for its motto: *Laudare, Benedicere, Praedicare*— "Praise, Bless, Preach." Before the Order sends its children into the apostolate it commits them to the worship of God, centering their lives around the liturgical hours of praise. The Order's spirit and apostolate become spiritually impoverished when the liturgy recedes into the background of Dominican thinking.

The Prayer of Sisters and Tertiaries

The spirituality of Dominican sisters and tertiaries, shared with a priestly and apostolic Order, is also liturgical. The little Office of the Blessed Mother which they recite fashions and molds them in the spirit of Mary, teaching them how to do everything in her, through her, by her, and for her. They contemplate the Mother of God, who, "kept in mind all these things, pondering them in her heart" (Luke, 2:19). They love souls because Mary, the mother of souls, loves them. They are anxious to save souls because she, the Mother of the Savior, wants to save them.

Dominican Saints and the Liturgy

The saints of the Order, sharing their Founder's love for the liturgy, were all men and women of prayer. Bernard Gui, who culled his information from those who had known St. Thomas Aquinas personally, describes the Saint's life of prayer:

> In St. Thomas the habit of prayer was extraordinarily developed. He seemed to be able to raise his mind to God as if the body's burden did not exist for him. At night, when our nature demands repose, he would rise after a short sleep and pray, lying prostrate on the ground. It was in those nights of prayer that he would learn what he would write or dictate in the daytime.

Bernard also writes of an incident that occurred on Passion Sunday at Naples when Thomas was celebrating Mass:

> He was seen by many persons present to become so deeply absorbed in the mystery that it was as if he had been admitted to a share in the sufferings of Christ. For a long time he remained as in a trance, his face bathed in tears. At last, some of the brethren came up and touched him and brought him back to himself, and he went on with the Mass. Afterwards, when asked by the brethren and by some of the knights who were his friends what had happened to him during that trance, he refused to tell them.

In another passage, Bernard records this important data:

> The Blessed Thomas had a particular devotion to the Sacrament of the Altar and no doubt the special profundity of his writings on this subject was

due to the same grace which enabled him to say
Mass so devoutly. This he did every day unless
prevented by sickness. After this he would hear,
and usually serve, another Mass said by his asso-
ciates or some other priest.

A Neapolitan Knight, Henry Caracciolo, showed in
the canonization process of the Angelic Doctor that his
love of the Mass equaled that of St. Dominic:

> We had often heard men speak of this religious as
> very upright, very pure and holy, a great con-
> templative and a man of prayer; and that he said
> his Mass daily and then assisted at another. If
> impeded from celebrating himself, he would hear
> two Masses, after which he studied, so that all
> his life was passed in reading, prayer, or study.

A profoundly significant episode in the life of St.
Catherine of Siena, related by Raymond of Capua, indi-
cated her great appreciation of the liturgy. Catherine did
not know how to read or write but was consumed by a
keen desire to recite the Divine Office. To satisfy this
longing, she determined to learn how to read. Raymond
describes the sequel:

> Catherine told me that when she decided to learn
> to read so that she could say the divine praises
> and the canonical hours, a friend of hers wrote the
> alphabet out and tried to teach it to her; but after
> spending many fruitless weeks over it, she de-
> cided not to waste any more time and turned to
> heavenly grace instead. One morning she knelt
> down and prayed to the Lord thus: "Lord", she
> said, "if you want me to learn to read so that I
> can say the psalms and sing your praises in the
> canonical hours, deign to teach me what I am not
> clever enough to learn myself. If not, thy will be
> done. I shall be quite content to remain in my
> ignorance and shall be able to spend more time
> in meditating on you in other ways."

Then a marvel happened—clear proof of God's power—for during this prayer she was divinely instructed so that when she got up she knew how to read any kind of writing quite easily and fluently, like the best reader in the world. When I realized it, I was quite flabbergasted, especially when I discovered that though she could read so fast, she could hardly spell the words. I believe that Our Lord meant this to be a sign of the miracle that had taken place.

From then on, Catherine began to hunt for books of the Divine Office to read the psalms and anthems and the other things fixed for the canonical hours.

Elsewhere, Raymond records how Christ would often visit Catherine: "He talked to her as one friend to another, so much so that she shyly confessed to me that they would say the psalms together, walking up and down the little room like two religious brothers saying their office." During these meetings when they came to the *Gloria Patri et Filio,* instead of saying *Filio,* Catherine would bow to the Lord and say *Tibi;* "Glory be to the Father and *to You* and to the Holy Spirit, Amen".

The Dominican Man of Prayer

The ambition to become a prayerful man must consume the Dominican. He should give scrupulous attention to his spiritual life, should devote himself especially to his prayers of obligation, faithfully attending choir, reciting the rosary, and making meditation. The Mass should be the cardinal point of his day. Convinced that prayer is more important than anything else he does, he should never push it into the background even when he has a busy day in the pulpit, a trying time in the confessional, counseling room, or classroom, or is engrossed in studying or correcting papers. Prayer sanctifies these active works, intersperses the day with recollection, and renews basic motivations.

But the Dominican is also an apostle and must leave his prayer from time to time to work for souls. When he does this, to some degree, he puts the blessings of the cloister behind him. The sister does likewise when she enters the classroom or the hospital ward. They expose their own spiritual life to temporary interruption. But this need not be dangerous if prayer dominates their lives, if they have taken the advice of St. Catherine seriously and constructed a cell in their hearts. If they live in this inner cell and are armed with the shield of faith, they can securely sally forth to do battle for souls. Fr. Bede Jarrett, himself a splendid example of the prayerful apostle, writes about the valor of the early friars who went forth from their priories in this spirit:

> They looked upon themselves as spiritual free-lances, tilting all the world over, from west to east, at every form of error and in defense of every truth. No monastic enclosure forbade their free movements, and the very choral obligation of chanted office was by the express command of Saint Dominic to be sacrificed whenever it prevented study or preaching. They took as their boast what Matthew of Paris used to say of them with scorn: "That the whole earth was their cell and the ocean was their cloister."

Not only have the friars had to carry the spirit of the cloister into the apostolate, but the apostolate has, in a measure, come to them in the cloister. The Dominican fathers have had to accomodate their religious life to the modern scene. They have had to abandon the midnight chanting of matins. The nuns in their monasteries still adhere to this rigorous schedule, as they did at Prouille in the days of their Founder, but the fathers can seldom do it. Often their day does not end until midnight. In the Middle Ages, the friars retired between seven and nine o'clock, depending on the season; by midnight they had had all the sleep they needed. Many of them did not take advantage of the permission to retire again after lauds. St. Antoninus and many another friar went to his books once the Office had ended.

The modern apostle must be available when the faithful come to him after work, regardless of how late they come or stay. The Constitutions wisely permit this fitting of the religious schedule and monastic observances to the apostolic life. This adjustment does not hurt the religious spirit of the priest when his life is one of prayer. Being faithful to his apostolate he is fulfilling the purpose of the Order. The zealous priest accomplishes this purpose in a contemplative spirit, seeking to bring the fruits of the cloister to men in the world. His spirit lives constantly with God in the cloister, speaking to him there; with God in the world, speaking to him in the cell of the heart; with God in souls, speaking to him in his children.

If a Dominican is not devoted to prayer and praise, he cannot contemplate; he cannot even hope to contemplate. Without prayer, he will never penetrate the truths of faith. Speaking of Our Lord's mysteries, St. Thomas writes:

> If anyone would diligently and piously consider the mysteries of the Incarnation, he would find such a profundity of wisdom that it would exceed all human knowledge . . . the wonderful meaning of this mystery is manifested more and more to him who piously ponders it (*IV Cont. Gent., c.* 54).

He puts the emphasis on pondering. A soul of praise must constantly be meditating on the truths of faith. Mental prayer is a major obligation of the Dominican. Meditating the truths of faith over a lifetime causes a man to penetrate their inner meaning. In a single period of meditation, the religious may feel that he has done very little. He may have succumbed to sleep. But even St. Dominic was at times overcome by exhaustion and dozed during his vigils. The religious should not be so discouraged at the difficulties of mental prayer that he abandons it, or concludes that it is worthless. To approach any prayer with sincere intention is always worthwhile. Perserance is the important thing. God rewards constant efforts; eventually he manifests himself to the faithful religious, giving him a deeper understanding of the truths of faith. "He who loves me will be loved by my Father, and I will love him and manifest myself to him" (John, 14:21). Sometimes the Holy Spirit sends his illuminations long after the period of formal prayer has passed. It may be in the thick of the apostolate that the priest hears his whisperings. He will not hear these soft-spoken promptings if he does not live in the atmosphere of prayer, if he has not made a cell in his own heart. Unless the Dominican has made the truths of faith his own, by living them, he cannot teach them with any fruit. Certainly, he can talk about them, preach eloquent sermons, please his audience, but if he is not prayerful, he will speak with words alone. But if he is a spiritual man, his prayer as well as his words will work for the good of souls, begging graces for them.

The Prayer of the Dominican Family

As the Church is a family, the Mystical Body of Christ, so also the Order of Preachers is a mystical family. Its members, numbered in thousands, are joined to their holy father, St. Dominic, and to one another by the bonds of profession. By birth men are related to their parents, brothers, and sisters by ties of blood. Religious profession joins the Dominican in a spiritual relationship with his Founder and all his children on earth, in purgatory, and in heaven. This union is closer than the bond of blood linking earthly parents and children because it is supernatural.

Just as Christ in heaven offers to the heavenly Father his own Sacrifice and the prayers of his Mystical Body, St. Dominic as the head of the Dominican family presents the corporate worship of the whole Order. Dominicans never pray as mere individuals but as members of a vast family, including 10,000 members of the First Order, 7,000 nuns of the Second Order, 51,000 sisters of Third Order religious communities, and the multitude of Tertiaries received publicly and privately into the Order. This great chorus of souls—each with the primary obligation of prayer; each contributing to the volume of praise the Order offers daily to the honor of the Holy Trinity—constitutes the Dominican symphony of love, worship and adoration.

Even when a friar prays privately or in the miniature choir of a small priory, he is standing spiritually in the ranks of his brothers and sisters who adore God throughout the world. Though his prayers may have been filled with involuntary distractions, if he has sincerely begun them and tried to ward off his distractions he may comfort himself with the thought that he has added to the Order's daily prayer-offering to God. Unwilled distractions do not deprive prayer begun with the right intention of the power to merit and petition effectively. However, as Saint Thomas points out, he who prays will not in that case receive the consolations of prayer (*Summa Theol.*, II—II, q. 83, a. 13, 15). Nevertheless, applying these principles of the Angelic Doctor, he may reflect that he has achieved the chief ends of prayer: adoration, reparation, thanksgiving, and petition. He has united his prayers to the chorus of praise that Dominican saints are constantly presenting as parts of the heavenly choir, to the prayers that his brothers and sisters everywhere, in priories, monasteries, convents and homes, are day after day putting into Dominic's hands to offer to God. The personal prayer of each member of the Order joins with the praise that rises to the Throne of God from all over the Dominican world.

The apostolate of the Friars Preachers cannot fructify unless priests and sisters have behind them their own prayers and those of the entire Order. When priests, brothers, and sisters fulfill their prayer obligations—daily Mass, Holy Communion, Office, Rosary, and meditation—they help the Order do its work. The Order does not exist apart from its members. It can only achieve its end if each member prays and works. St. Dominic attached such importance to the corporate worship of the Order that he founded a special branch for the sole purpose of praying. "The nuns of the Sacred Order of Preachers," their Constitutions state, "constitute a religious Order . . . the members of which . . . strive after Christian perfection and by means of that perfection implore for the labors of their brethren abundant fruit in holiness." Father Gerald Vann elaborated beautifully on this duty of the contemplative Dominican nun:

> As Adam needed and was given a helpmate like to himself, so—the analogy is Père Cormier's—the first Order needed and was given a helpmate to share its work and life, and a helpmate like to itself because stamped with the same family spirit, the spirit of Dominic. The convents would be the Order's centres of energy . . .

What is true of the nun is true of all the other members of the Order. They cannot devote themselves as constantly as she to actual prayer but as men and women of prayer, priests, laybrothers, sisters, and tertiaries constantly implore God's blessings on the Order's apostolic work everywhere in the world.

When the Dominican prays, he is the first to benefit. His prayer will make him a fervent, intimate friend of God. He also helps his fellow Dominican and all his neighbors everywhere. The prayerful Dominican saves more souls by prayer and contemplation than by words and action.

When Dominicans chant their Office, St. Dominic stands in spirit among them as he did 700 years ago at Bologna. He goes from side to side encouraging them to put their whole heart in it. When they listen to him, they place their prayers in his hands. In turn, he bows toward the Holy Trinity, offering the combined homage and adoration of the entire mystical body of Friars Preachers.

ST. DOMINIC AT STUDY

Chapter VI

DOMINICAN LIFE

is

DOCTRINAL

Teaching and defending the faith in the pulpit is the apostolate of the Order of Preachers. The Order has widened this primary apostolate to include teaching, and other ways of communicating truth. The classroom and the press are important channels of Dominican activity. Teaching the truth in any way whatever makes the Dominican merciful: one who "instructs the ignorant," and "counsels the doubtful." The Constitutions directly refer to this apostolate of mercy.

> Our Order is known to have been founded from the beginning especially for preaching and the salvation of souls. Wherefore our study ought to aim principally at this that we might be useful to the souls of our neighbors. Intimately connected with this proper end is the teaching and defense of the truth of the Catholic faith both verbally in the schools and in much writing.

The special end of the nuns of the Order is "to implore for the labors of their brethren abundant fruit in holiness." The pursuit of this end fulfills several of the spiritual works of mercy: one of them directly, when the nuns pray for their brothers and sisters who are engaged in the active apostolate; and the others indirectly, when through the graces they implore for their brethen they share in the instruction of the ignorant and participate in counseling the doubtful.

Dominican sisters have made further extensions of the Order's apostolate of mercy. They not only teach but have undertaken the care of the sick and orphans. The mercy of the sisters is immediately evident from the opening chapter of their Constitutions:

> The principal and essential end of our congregation is the personal sanctification of the sisters. The secondary or special end is the education of Catholic youth, and/or the care of orphans, the nursing of the sick, the conducting of retreat houses, foreign missions and catechetical and social work.

A sister in the classroom or caring for orphans teaches the children entrusted to her. A good nurse or social worker is teaching all the time. These sisters teach their charges how to find Christ, how to know him, and how to love him.

Teaching involves study. The Constitutions place "the assiduous study of sacred truth" among the essential means of achieving the Order's end. Such devotion to truth gives a specific, particular flavor to the Dominican way of doing things. Humbert of Romans places our study in proper perspective: "Study is not the end of our Order, but is extremely necessary to secure its twofold end, namely, preaching and the salvation of souls. For without study neither can be achieved."

St. Dominic had a deep appreciation of learning,

study, and teaching. So profound was his love for the truths of the faith that he spent his entire life proclaiming them and was anxious to die for them. He wanted to spread the truths of faith to the ends of the earth. He so valued revealed truth that he always carried the Gospel of St. Matthew and the Epistles of St. Paul. He "often admonished and exhorted the friars of the Order by word and letter to study constantly in the Old and the New Testament." As a student at Palencia, he was so anxious to begin the study of theology that he hastened through the liberal arts course.

> When he felt that he had sufficiently learned the arts, he stopped studying them, as if he were reluctant to spend any longer time in these less fruitful studies, and turned to the study of theology. He spent four years in these sacred studies during which he drank avidly and incessantly from the streams of Sacred Scripture. So indefatigable was his zeal to learn and retain tenaciously the truth of those things which he was learning that he would spend almost whole nights without sleep. . . . God added to him the grace of knowledge so that he might be ready not only to drink milk but to probe with humility the secrets of difficult questions and swallow the meat of inquiry with ease.

As this text indicates, study of theology in the medieval schools was study of Sacred Scripture. The master of theology was the master of the sacred page, that is, the master of Sacred Scripture. It was the bachelor of theology's duty to expound the sacred books textually. To the master was reserved a profound doctrinal interpretation of the text. It is to St. Thomas' tenure as master of theology that we owe his commentaries on the books of the Old and New Testaments. When St. Dominic prompted the early friars to study the Old and New Testaments constantly, he was telling them to study their theology—to know the truths of the faith, to drink them from the very font.

In setting a contemplative and apostolic end for his sons and daughters, the Founder gave them duties that cannot be fulfilled unless they study and proclaim the truth. When Bishop Foulques of Toulouse approved the Order of Preachers as a diocesan institute in 1215, Dominic had already impressed this doctrinal character on his Order. In the Bishop's foundation charter we read: "We institute the Order of Preachers to stamp out heresy and vice, to teach the faith, and to establish men in a life of sound morality." The Constitutions indicates these same ends: "Our Order was founded from the beginning for preaching and the salvation of souls." It is impossible to do what the charter of 1215 proposed or what the Constitutions command without study.

The Saint wanted the best education possible for his children. Soon after Bishop Foulques had issued his charter, the Founder enrolled his first sons for a course of theology at the cathedral school of Toulouse under Master Alexander of Stavensby. Early in 1216 the friars began to put up their first priory, that of St. Romanus in Toulouse. Jordan of Saxony, our only authority for this event, says everything he has to say about it in one short sentence. He doesn't say how big it was, whether it was made of bricks, stone, or wood, or what street it was on. Only one thing stood out in his mind as worth recording: " . . . it had cells for studying."

In August, 1217, St. Dominic sent eight of his small band of sixteen to Paris. They went there, John of Spain informs us in the canonization process, "to study, to preach, and to found a priory." They did just that, establishing St. Jacques priory and enrolling at the University of Paris, the mother university of the world. In 1218, Dominic founded another house at Bologna, the seat of the second university of Europe. The next year, when he visited Paris, he engaged the services of John of St. Albans, master of theology, to give his courses at the Dominican priory. This act incorporated St. Jacques into the University and gave it official status, making it the first house of studies of any religious Order at the first university of Europe. In 1220, when the King of Castle founded the University of Palencia, the Founder sent friars to that city. In the same year, the municipal authorities of Montpellier in southern France began a university, and he founded a priory there. In 1221, at the second general chapter of the Order, he sent thirteen friars to Oxford to open a house at the university, the third great intellectual center of Christendom. As Father Jarret rightly remarks:

> The main point to be noted . . . is the true objective of the friars on their arrival [in England] was Oxford. They halted at Cantebury and London, but it is clear that they as yet made no foundation in either of these places. This is a noticeable fact, and it supplies the keynote of the Dominican ideal. These friars arrived in England, strange and unknown, their dress unfamiliar, their fashion of life new and so far untried in these islands. They were welcomed in the ecclesiastical capital of the country, but they passed on. They arrived at the political capital where dwelt the government and the commercial center; but this too they left. It was the intellectual capital of England that they "finally reached." They made their first settlement, not near the Primate, not the King but at the University, for in the Middle Ages it was a common saying that there were three great powers in Christendom, the *Sacerdotium,* the *Imperium,* and the *Studium,* and the greatest of these was the *Studium.*

It was quite in keeping with this tradition that the American Dominicans transferred their *studium* from 'Ohio to Washington, D.C., soon after the Catholic University of America opened its doors. As at Paris, the Friars Preachers were the first of the Orders to establish themselves at the new university, contributing both professors and students to the new institution. This coming

of the friars was of tremendous significance both for the
Province of St. Joseph and the university. His Eminence,
James Cardinal Gibbons, in an after-dinner address on
the occasion of the Order's Seven-Hundredth Anniversary,
1916, expressed his gratitude for the timely support the
Order brought to the university by establishing its House
of Studies just off campus:

> I shall confine my remarks to what the Order
> of Saint Dominic has done for the Catholic
> University of America. For the Dominicans have
> given a striking proof of such sympathetic
> friendship by rallying loyally to the support
> of the University in its hour of need. A hundred
> years from now, doubtless, the foundation of
> the University will be conceded to have been
> the greatest Catholic achievement of our times:
> and to the Fathers of St. Dominic will be justly
> accorded no small measure of the credit for
> its success. . . .
> The University, as you know, has had its dark
> days—its days of trial and tribulation, when its
> very existence was threatened and the period
> of its usefulness seemed to be at an end. The
> clouds were, indeed, dark, for all appeared to be
> in a state of dissolution. It was just at this
> moment—a moment of almost despair on the part
> of the American hierarchy—that the Fathers of
> Saint Dominic came like brave soldiers to the
> rescue. They came to express their confidence
> in the University and their conviction that it must
> continue and must succeed. To all interested in
> the University their coming gave a moral support
> the value of which cannot be overestimated. To
> me, the chancellor, it was as a ray of light shin-
> ing out in the blackness of night. Had they not
> come when they did, we should have lacked a
> sorely needed moral support without which the
> University might never have survived. The group
> of religious Orders that has now gathered about
> the University and is constantly being augmented,

or are gathering, has but strengthened the confidence and confirmed the assurance given by the optimism of the Dominicans. . . .

This imposing array of facts demonstrates clearly the importance the Friars Preachers attach to learning. St. Dominic wanted his men near the universities where they could learn the sacred sciences under the best theologians of Europe. When he sent his sons to school it was clear that some of them would become teachers. That was one of the reasons for sending them. The Constitutions required every priory to have its professors as well as prior. But over and above that, it was impossible to take a degree at the medieval university without teaching, which was part of the training. It is not surprising to see the Dominicans at Paris acquiring their first professional chair in 1229 and their second in 1230, less than a decade after the Saint's death. He was such a practical man that he put into the Constitutions at the first general chapter detailed regulations governing study, the duties of the master of students, and the student life of the friar. They permitted the brethren "to read, write, pray, sleep, and also, those who wish, to stay up at night to study" in their cells. The novice master was instructed to teach the novices, "how they ought to be so intent on study that day and night, at home or on the road, they read or meditate something."

This was something new in the history of religious Orders. For the first time in a thousand years of monastic history, a religious Order incorporated into its rule sections dealing with the academic life. A deep significance attaches to this fact. By writing these laws into the Constitutions, St. Dominic sanctified study and learning. The regulations dealing with study stand side by side, on the same footing, with the rubrics dealing with the conventual Mass, the Divine Office, prayer, and preaching. These laws made study a sacred obligation for every Dominican, an obligation that binds with the same force that prayer binds. Saints Albert and Thomas symbolize the sanctifying power and the sacred nature of learning pursued for the love of souls; the Church has declared the first the patron saint of those who study the natural sciences, the second the patron of all Catholic schools.

In the Order's life there is no break in religious continuity when the friar steps from the chapel into the study room or classroom. In each place he fulfills a religious obligation. A Dominican is not less a religious when he leaves the choir. Study is an indipensable preparation for his spiritual life, preaching, teaching, and apostolate. For the nun, study is essential "for the devout and constant contemplation of Our Lord, Creator, Redeemer, and Sanctifier." For the sister, it is necessary for her personal sanctification and for teaching or nursing.

The Order's history shows that its members have been loyal to this intellectual heritage. Great schools have dotted the Dominican map: the College of St. Gregory at Valladolid, St. Stephen at Salamanca, St. Thomas at the Minerva and its sucessor, the University of St. Thomas in Rome, the Biblical School at St. Stephen's in Jerusalem.

In the New World, before Harvard began classes in 1636, Spainish friars had built a chain of colleges and universities that stretched from the West Indies, through Mexico, into South America, and across the Pacific to the Philippine Islands. Santo Domingo, Havana, Puerto Rico, Mexico, Caracas, Bogotà had Dominican colleges or universities awarding higher degrees. The University of Santo Tomàs, founded at Manila in 1611, and still operated by Dominicans, is the oldest University in Asia. Today it has more than 30,000 students.

The force of this intellectual tradition led the American Dominicans in Kentucky, under the leadership of Father Fenwick, to set up a college as soon as they established a priory. St. Thomas College was the first Catholic college west of the Alleghanies and the third any place in the United States. This frontier institution failed after twenty years. The fathers founded two other colleges that had short lives, but finally succeeded at Providence, Rhode Island. American Dominicans have become increasingly involved in education. The 17,000 American Dominican Sisters in the United States, most of whom are teachers and deeply aware of the Order's doctrinal apostolate, have founded and staff twenty-four colleges and surely this is not yet the end.

The modern intellectual apostolate demands that teachers be trained academically. This was not so necessary in 1850, or even as late as 1920. But in the latter half of the twentieth century it is essential. If Catholic schools are to keep pace and have their place in the intellectual world, then teachers must be carefully prepared. The construction of college buildings, libraries, and research centers at Dominican priories and motherhouses and on Dominican campuses is a development that our Founder would approve.

He did not want the Order to stagnate. "Seed which is hoarded becomes rotten; when scattered it germinates," was his dictum when he daringly sent his sons to every corner of Europe to open new frontiers in the history of religious Orders. Dominicans must keep moving and remain abreast of the times. If Dominic were living today, he would make changes and adaptations to keep his Order in harmony with twentieth-century developments. We know that he would do this because he wrote the Constitutions in such a way that needed changes can always be made. Old laws can be abolished, new laws put in their place, and whole new sections added to the Constitutions by using the machinery of the general chapters.

Keeping the Order up-to-date is not only in agreement with our heritage and constant tradition, but is what the Church expects of its Orders. His Eminence Cardinal Larraona, Secretary of the Congregation for Religious and the Pope's legate at the 1956 Conference of Religious at Notre Dame, told the assembled delegates that they must make the changes necessary to keep their apostolates modern. "By doing what your founders would do in your place, what they would do if they were living in your times, you will continue their work." The master general and the general chapter have the right to make adaptations of existing law in St. Dominic's name. When the master general gives his blessing, he gives the blessing of St. Dominic. Michael Cardinal Browne (then Master General) told American Dominicans when he was in the United States that he spoke in the name of our Founder, that what he said was what "our holy Father Dominic would say were he here with you."

A Dominican should rejoice when the Order updates its apostolate. St. Dominic was an "up-to-the-minute" man of the thirteenth century. With the foundation of the Order, he met the problems of his day. These problems included bishops who did not preach, priests who did not instruct, people who did not know their faith. Schools founded in every one of the Order's priories, in accordance with the Constitutions, soon formed an elite priesthood, preachers who were well-prepared to preach, confessors who knew how to admonish and advise, spiritual directors who could lead souls to sanctity, and learned theologians who were the theological leaders of the Church. Little wonder that popes and bishops drafted the friars, despite their reluctance, for all kinds of services. Well into modern times, when they wanted legates to go on embassies or to do special kinds of ecclesiastical work, they turned to the friars. Today, when secular clergy and religious are almost universally well-instructed, Dominicans are not called on so often to undertake these extraordinary duties.

St. Dominic would approve anything we do to meet modern conditions, provided we do not change the character of the Order. The basic problem is the same in all ages, that is, to teach the faith. Our Lord says to every age of apostles: "Go therefore, and make disciples of all nations . . . teaching them to observe all that I have commanded you" (Matt. 28: 19-20). But the message of salvation must be expressed in the language of the day. No Dominican today preaches like the friars of 700 years ago; he does not teach like they did. Perhaps they taught better, certainly St. Thomas did, but the methods were medieval, today they must be modern. The twentieth century Dominican must be a twentieth-century man. St. Paul said:

> I have become to the Jews a Jew that I might gain those under the Law; to those without the Law, as one without the Law . . . that I might gain those without the Law. To the weak I became weak, that I might gain the weak. I became all things to all men, that I might save all. I do all things for the sake of the Gospel, that I may be made partaker thereof (I Cor. 9:20-23).

The Dominican must say: 'I became an American to the Americans, that I might gain the Americans; a twentieth-century priest, that I might gain twentieth-century men." He must understand the thought-patterns of his fellow-citizen, learn how he thinks, how he lives, how he is trained. The friar must take the eternal truths and adapt them, particularize them, to meet the needs of this decade. That is how St. Dominic, St. Albert, and St. Thomas acted. When the medieval Church sought a solution for the great ecclesiastical problems of the thirteenth-century, St. Dominic pointed the way with a new kind of religious Institute, a mixed contemplative and apostolic Order. When the theologians of Europe floundered in their attempt to cope with the Eastern learning that was flooding the West for the first time after many centuries, Albert the Great, with the insight of genius, divined the situation and probed the needs of his time. He realized that neither flight from Aristotle, prohibition of his works, nor electic choice of his texts was the right solution. Christian thought must enter into this heritage and make it its own. But it remained for St. Thomas to complete the work. Albert prepared the way but never constructed an integral system of philosophical and theological thought. Thomas cut through the gropings and hesitations of his predecessors to construct the first system of philosophy since the Greeks and the first system of theology since Augustine. In his writings, Thomas dealt with every problem of the day. He was meek and mild, never raised his voice to an adversary, but he was a Christian gladiator who spent all the years of his professorship in the arena. He beat out the sword of Thomism in the forge of battle, on the anvil of combat, under the fire of enemies. Vital, contemporary problems were at issue in every campaign.

The superficial modern reader, not knowing the background of Thomas' life, might conclude from reading his works that these problems were very far afield indeed. But as a master of theology at Paris, Naples, and Rome, Thomas was in the thick of all the controversies that were waging at the time. His was a constant dialogue, a continuous encounter with the best minds of the day. In his *opuscula* especially, he handled current problems.

A century ago, Père Lacordaire· lived a similar life in the arena. He was alive to the needs of nineteenth-century Europe as few men of his time. It is significant of the modernity and flexibility of the Dominican Order that when the ultra-modern Lacordaire, one of the founders of Liberal-Catholicism, decided to enter a religious Order he became a Dominican. He had studied the religious life in its every phase with the intent of embracing it and was well able to explain why he brought an old Order back to France instead of founding a new one of his own:

> Even were God to give us the power of creating a religious Order, we feel sure, after much reflection, that we could find nothing newer, nothing better adapted to our own time and to our own wants than the rule of St. Dominic. It has nothing ancient about it but its history, and we

do not see any necessity of torturing our minds for the simple pleasure of dating from yesterday.

Père Joseph Lagrange met the needs of the Church at the turn of the century with his pioneer work on the Bible. He answered the attacks of the Higher Critics by stealing their weapons. He was so far ahead of other Catholic biblical scholars that only half a century later did they begin to catch up with him. The Order is proud of his work and the school he founded—St. Stephen's Biblical School in Jerusalem, one of the world's foremost center of Scripture studies. Its professors are in the front rank of biblical scholarship. The work of Père Henri Pire for refugees in our post-war world is so well-known that it need not be described.

St. Dominic would approve the work the Order is doing today. He approves of Dominican sisters teaching in classrooms of all schools from kindergarten to university. In the thirteenth century, our fathers taught only the sacred sciences in houses of study and universities. There were no other schools in that day except law schools and the schools of the guilds. Women seldom received a formal education. Today every young man and woman needs an education. It is absolutely normal for Dominicans to teach the youth of the day. It was normal in the thirteenth century to teach the sacred sciences to clerics, practically the only youth who received an education. It is certainly laudable today to teach the variety of studies that the young people of our day need—religion or theology, mathematics or music, biology or nuclear physics. Whether the Dominican teaches in school or in the hospital room, he can always say: "I am a child of St. Dominic." All truth is Christian, because all truth comes from God. All these subjects are necessary today to fashion the whole man, the integral member of the Mystical Body of Christ destined for heaven. All education is directed toward that ultimate destiny. Dominicans of today must somehow be engaged in the field of education to achieve the Dominican apostolate—the salvation of souls through preaching.

The Sources of the Dominican Apostolate

How can the Dominican prepare for preaching and teaching in the Dominican way? He must do it in St. Dominic's way, seeking to know Christ, to be united with him in the bonds of closest friendship. It was as a contemplative united to Christ that Dominic gained the grace of the apostle; a thought to which Dante, the poet-theologian of medieval Italy, gave lovely expression:

> . . . And there was born
> The loving minion of the Christian faith
> The Hallow'd wrestler, gentle to his own,
> And to his enemies terrible . . .

> And I speak of him as the laborer
> Whom Christ in His own garden chose to be
> His helpmate. Messenger he seem'd and friend,
> Fast-knit to Christ; and the first love he show'd
> Was after the first counsel that Christ gave.

> Then with sage doctrine and good will to help,
> Forth on his great apostleship he fared,
> Like torrent bursting from a lofty vein;
> And dashing 'gainst the stocks of heresy,
> Smoke fiercest where resistance was most stout.
>   (*Paradiso, XII*)

It is a "friend, fast knit to Christ" that Dominic became his "laborer", "helpmate", "messenger". Before preaching Christ Crucified, Dominic spent long hours contemplating him:

> He would remain before the altar or in the chapter room with gaze fixed on the Crucified One, looking upon him with perfect attention. He genuflected frequently, again and again. . . . Thus there was formed in our holy father St. Dominic a great confidence in God's mercy towards himself, all sinners, and for the persever-

ance of the younger brethren whom he sent forth
to preach to souls.

Beneath the Crucifix he merited the "double spirit" of
contemplation and action, the grace to take upon himself, in the words of the heavenly Father in the *Dialogues*
of St. Catherine of Siena, ". . . the office of the Word,
my only-begotten Son. And at once he appeared before the world as an apostle, sowing my word with much
truth and light. He was a light that I placed in the
world by means of Mary."

All saintly Dominicans became apostles at the feet
of Christ. St. Thomas was devoted to the Blessed Sacrament; St. Albert to the Eucharistic Heart. Bl. Henry
Suso carved the sacred Name of Jesus on his breast. St.
Catherine of Siena accomplished everything "in the Blood
of Christ". It was Christ, the Divine Truth, "God of God,
Light of Light", whom they sought in their devotions.
The Friar Preacher must become so wrapped up in Christ
that he can speak of nothing else. With St. Paul he
must say: "I determined not to know anything among
you, except Jesus Christ and him crucified" (I Cor. 2:2).
As a man of prayer, he will preach and teach "Christ
and him curcified" no matter where he preaches or
teaches, because in his own life he has become "another
Christ."

The Dominican, therefore, must prepare to preach
and teach by becoming a contemplative. Contemplation
must be primary in his life; he must be a contemplative
committed to the apostolate. It is his ideal to contemplate
and to have the fruits of his contemplation, of his life
of prayer, flow into his apostolate. His apostolic work
will bear fruit to the extent that he is personally holy.
His apostolate must be "shaped in the sanctuary, he
choir, and the cloister." The Dominican's contemplation
must be Christlike and redemptive. He must see Christ
in those who hear him, in those he teaches, in those he
nurses. As the early Christians put it: "He who sees

his neighbor sees God." Each listener, each student, each
patient has been redeemed by Christ, in a sense, is Christ.
The Dominican apostle must see Christ in each human
being, whether an energetic child or an aged sick person,
even the most annoying, the one who tries his patience
most.

The Dominican contemplative preparing for preaching and teaching must never feel that time given to prayer
is time stolen from the apostolate. Nor must he regret
it when duty calls him from the choir to the classroom or
the pulpit. His prayer and study are not sealed off in
separate compartments; rather, there is a constant ebb
and flow: from prayer to study, from study to prayer. He
must never become an "intellectual", in current slang, an
"egg-head," a person who has no use for prayer and the
things of the spirit; one who is all head and no heart.
It is sometimes said that it is Dominican to be an "intellectual". It is, but not with quotation marks. A Dominican
intellectual is first a man of prayer; he is a prayerful
intellectual. Prayer seasons and warms his learning, gives
it life, frees it from the cobwebs and dust of ponderous
tomes.

The two most outstanding teachers of the Order have
studied and taught as contemplatives. St. Albert, the
greatest scholar of his generation, was also a saint, and
formed a saint. Here is how Thomas of Cantimprè, one
of Albert's Dominican students, describes his teacher:

> As a student over a long period, I have seen
> and noted that almost every day for many years
> when Master Albert was regent of theology, he
> so devoted himself to prayer, day and night, that
> he recited the 150 psalms of David every day.

Some modern authors, commenting on this passage, say
that Contimprè must have made a mistake; he meant the
seven penitential psalms, not the psalter. But he was
a learned friar; he knew much better than we do, from
personal experience, what the seven penitential psalms

and the psalter are. There is only one psalter and it is composed of the 150 psalms of David. But Albert was not distracted by the noises and diversions of modern life. Then Cantimprè continued: "He dedicated himself to the canonical hours, his lectures, and disputations." In fact, he used a word that drawing-room minds might consider inelegant. Where I said "dedicated", Cantimprè said "sweated"—*Sudavit*. Albert "sweated over the canonical hours, his lectures, and disputations." It means being supremely attentive and painstaking. Then Cantimprè concluded: "Is it any wonder that such a man, advancing in such a holy and upright way, should make more than human progress in virtue?" William of Tocco also wrote about Albert in his life of St. Thomas telling us that, "this wonderful master offered his students simultaneously the knowledge of wisdom and the example of a holy life"—the perfect teacher.

Perhaps it was from Albert's example that St. Thomas and larning. Leo XIII, proclaiming him Patron of Catholic Schools, found that he possessed these two qualities in an eminent degree: "The Angelic Doctor is great no less in his virtue and holiness than in his doctrine. Virtue is the most excellent preparation for training the powers of the mind and for acquiring learning."

The contemporaries of St. Thomas were impressed by his habit of turning to prayer when he ran into difficulties in his studies. Reginald of Priverno, his companion for many years, made the following statement to one of his classes shortly after the funeral of his master:

> My dear brothers, while my master lived I was prevented by him from revealing the wonderful things I know about him. Among these was this, that his knowledge, which was amazing beyond that of others, was not the result of human genius but of prayer. For always before he

studied, disputed, lectured, wrote, or dictated, he would have recourse to the help of prayer, begging with tears to be shown the truth about the divine things he had to investigate. By the merit of this prayer, the things that were doubtful before he began to pray, became, after his prayer, wonderfully clear to him.

Reginald cited this striking example of such recourse to prayer:

On another occasion it was an obscure text on Isaias that puzzled him. So much so that for many days he could not get any further with it, though he prayed and fasted assiduously, begging for light to see into the prophet's mind. At last, one night when he had stayed up to pray, his companion overheard him speaking, as it seemed, with other persons in the room. Though what was being said the companion could not make out, nor did he recognize the other voices. Then these fell silent and he heard Thomas caling. "Reginald, my son, get up and bring a light and the commentary on Isaias. I want you to write for me."

(St. Thomas had a difficult handwriting which was regular but hard to read. A trained paleographer of the Leonine Commission has estimated that it takes six months to learn how to read it well. After his first ten years as professor, St. Thomas stopped writing his works. He made outlines and dictated to his secretaries, one of whom was Reginald).

So Reginald rose and began to take down the dictation, which ran so clearly that it was as if the master were reading aloud from a book under his eyes. This continued for an hour, and then Thomas said, "Now go back to bed, son: there is little time left for sleep." (But Reginald wouldn't go. He refused to move until Thomas would tell him who had been speaking with him.) At last Thomas said, while tears ran down his cheeks: "My son, you have seen the distress I have suffered lately because of that text which I have only now finished explaining. I could not understand it, and I begged Our Lord to help me, and tonight He sent His blessed Apostles to me, Peter and Paul, whose intercession I had also begged for; and they have spoken to me and told me all I desired to know. But now, in God's name, never tell anyone else of this as long as I live. I have told you only because you urge me so strongly."

If the Dominican wants to teach in the Dominican way, he must do so with a sense of mission. The word "mission" comes from Latin: *mittere,* to send. He must teach as one sent by the Church. It is true that only the bishops officially teach. They send the priests. And just as the bishop cannot do it all alone but sends priests, so priests cannot do it alone, but need the sisters. Sisters are not official teachers in the sense that bishops and priests are, but they collaborate with the priests, teaching with a definite commission from the Church herself to do so.

Members of the Order must enter their apostolate with a love for truth. All truth is one, but in our poor human way we can only understand it by dividing it into subjects of study. All truth is a reflection of God, the first Truth. All truth comes from him and leads back to him. Love for truth must permeate the entire life of the Friar Preacher. His pursuit of truth is the heart of his preparation for the apostolate; it is the burden of his message when he preaches, teaches, counsels, or instructs. It conditions all he does or says: "For out of the abundance of the heart the mouth peaks" (Matt. 12:34).

When the Dominican rises from prayer and ascends the pulpit or enters the classroom, he must go as Christ went into the roads of Palestine, as the Apostle went into the highways of the world, as Dominic went through the Albigensian country and across the plains of Lombardy—"seeking souls, preaching the word, being urgent in season, out of season; reproving, entreating, rebuking with all patience and teaching" (II Tim. 2:2).

That was how St. Dominic wanted his children to preach and teach, imitating his own indomitable spirit. John of Spain gives us a graphic description of that spirit:

> Filled with compassion, he most ardently desired his neighbor's salvation. He himself preached often and in every way possible exhorted the brethren to preach. He sent them out to preach, begging and urging them to be solicitous for the salvation of souls. Confiding greatly in God, he sent even the ungifted ones to preach, saying to them: "Go confidently, for the Lord will give you the word of preaching and be with you, and nothing shall be wanting to you." They went out and it happened to them just as he had said.

Chapter VII

DOMINICAN LIFE
is
FRATERNAL

The end of the Order of Friars Preachers is contemplation fructifying in the apostolate. Among the means to achieve the end are the three vows of obedience, chastity, and poverty and the regular life with its monastic observances. The words "regular life" refer to the religious life lived in community.

The heart of Dominican life is brotherly love. In community life this fraternal love is given full opportunity to manifest itself. There can be no religious Order, no fraternal love among brethren, without life in common. All the members of the Order are called to live a life together, sharing the same food, the same furniture, the same facilities, the same kind of clothing. St. Augustine writes in his Rule:

> Call not anything your own, but let all things be held in common. Food and clothing shall

be distributed to each one of you by your
superior, not in equal measure to all, because
all are not equally strong, but rather to each
one according to his need. For thus we read in
the Acts of the Apostles: "they held all things
in common and distribution was made to each
according as anyone had need" (Acts 2:45).

Value of the Common Life

The common life makes many contributions to the
temporal and spiritual well-being of the member of a
religious Order. It brings him the fellowship of confreres,
instruction, formation, and direction in the religious life,
a congenial atmosphere for living virtuously, economic
security, the example of others, collaboration in the apostolate, the assurance that his work will continue once he is
incapable of further effort, and above all fraternal love
and support.

Even the onerous aspects of community life—submis-
sion to authority, sacrifice of personal will, bearing with
the defects of others—bring with them opportunities for
mortification and sacrifice. We shall pass over most of
these benefits and speak chiefly of the function of the
community life in promoting contemplation and the apostolate, the two great ends of the Order. The sacrificial side
of common life and monastic observances we shall examine especially in the next chapter.

Community life is not now as rigorous as it was in
earlier centuries. Religious today have many things, their
religious habits and books, for example, allocated for their
personal use. They receive sufficient food, necessary furniture, and adequate medical care when needed. Most
religious, coming from middle class families, are not ac-
customed to luxuries and do not find these aspects of the
common life very trying. They did not have luxuries before they came to religion and are now content with very
little. But though they find their material needs so well
taken care of, they should not underestimate the impor-

tance of the community life, which helps them to advance spiritually. Even though life in common gives oportunity to commit faults, it offers much more room for love and sacrifice.

Community life goes much deeper than holding material things in common. More important is the sharing of the spiritual riches of soul and mind: the sharing of obedience and chastity, of virtues and talents, of all that the religious has and is. The common life both protects these things and places them at the service of the Order. What other people get paid for, the religious does for nothing. He does it for the love of God and for his community, making his time and talents available to the Church. This is not a little thing. Educational associations recognize the contributed services of the religious teacher as a living endowment. For example, it is estimated that the priests at Providence College contribute to Catholic education by their teaching the equivalent of a million dollar endowment. Our schools do not have extensive financial endowments but such consecrated services are far superior.

Community Life and Vows

Community life protects the chastity of religious through the vow, the habit, the enclosure, and silence. It gives the safeguards of law, obedience, mortification and sacrifice. It relieves the friar of the burdens of a family so that he might give himself more constantly to prayer and works for neighbor. Priests and sisters may not be as free to spend time in prayer as they would like, but, nevertheless, they have much more leisure for spiritual concerns than the mothers and fathers of families who can seldom attend daily Mass and receive Communion. Even though the Dominican spends so many hours in apostolic works or in the classroom, his vows give him much freedom and leisure to devote himself to God.

Obedience, the most important vow, protects the religious from the misuse of his talents, brings him the guid-

ance of superiors, ensures him constancy of purpose and
steady progress toward perfection. Obedience causes a
great holocaust of consecrated lives to send up the smoke
of sacrifice from the thousands of Dominican priories,
monasteries, motherhouses, and convents that cover the
map of the world. Obedience is also the key to the apostolic use of talents. It provides sustained direction and
united action in pursuing the works of the community.
Religious of ordinary talent, banded together under obedience, gain great effectiveness and accomplish works that
could never have been done alone. Supported by the
strength and ability of fellow religious, they work more
effectively and with greater endurance. Furthermore, no
individual is the best judge of his own powers and abilities. When looking at himself, he finds it hard to be im-
partial; he either overrates or underrates his ability, and
is in danger of misusing talents through personal whim,
selfishness, or vainglory. Along this path lies frustration.
The religious avoids this danger by laying his talents at
the feet of his superior who will direct him in their use.

Even the most talented religious places his abilities
at the disposal of the community. The prior may be
mediocre in comparison with this superior person. Yet
despite his surrender, the talented religious does not stifle
his personality when he obeys. Though his prior may be
inferior to him in talent, he is superior in rank because
he is God's representative. He interprets God's will for
his subject. This does not mean that a superior never
makes a mistake, that everything he does is wise and pru-
dent. Experience shows that this is far from true. Every
human being, however gifted, makes mistakes; some make
more than others. But the religious never makes a mistake
in obeying. God does not want the prior to make mistakes
in guiding the community, but he tolerates them. He does
not work miracles to prevent them, just as he did not
work a miracle to stop the betrayal by Judas. But once
the act had been done, it was the heavenly Father's will
that Christ allow himself to be taken by the soldiers sent

with Judas to arrest him. Christ used the betrayal to bring to mankind the infinite fruit of the Redemption. When the prior makes a mistake, God does not approve it, but he does permit it. Obedience to the erroneous command is God's will for the subject. The obedient religious takes the order, uses it, and brings spiritual good from it, perhaps the fruit of patience and suffering, but fruit for himself and souls.

It is God's will that the subject obey in everything except sin. No superior, not even the Pope, may oblige religious to do something that is sinful. Even though the vow of obedience binds only to commands which are in accordance with the Rule and the Constitutions, there is also the filial obedience which arises from the common life. In his community the superior is father and has a dominative power which calls for obedience over a field far wider than that covered by the vow alone. A perfect religious not only values the vow but prizes, and much more highly, the virtue of obedience.

Obedience has always been a strong virtue in the Order of Preachers. It is the only vow that Dominicans mention explicitly in their profession formula. Unlike some religious, they do not take the vow to obey the rule, but a person, a person representing God. Dominican obedience has a personal quality that it does not have in every Order. It is the keystone of Dominican existence. It is not negative but positive. It is the fulfillment of personality because it makes the religious like the Only-Begotten Son of God who was obedient unto death. Imitation is one of the finest tributes we can render to Christ. He was obedient, not only to his heavenly Father, but also to Mary and Joseph. He obeyed Pilate, Herod, the High Priest, and his executioners.

Community Life — A School of Contemplation

Community life, built on the three vows, enables Dominicans to work for the purposes of the Order. The common life of the priory, monastery, or convent is a school of contemplation. If the friar is on a lower level of prayer, living in a community prepares him for higher prayer, because it demands the practice of virtue, especially fraternal charity.

It is impossible to live day by day, year after year, in community, standing beside the same person in choir, sitting beside him in the refectory, without being tried in many ways. Then there are the bells that keep ringing, summoning the religious to stop one thing and take up another. Said one sister: "One day I counted thirty-four bells from 5 A.M. to 9 P.M. There is nothing but bells, bells, and more bells." Such reguarity is one of the greatest mortifications of religious life.

St. John of the Cross writes that the common life not only consoles and supports the religious but also tries and tests him. St. Therese of Lisieux tells of the annoyance she suffered from the nun who constantly rattled her rosary. That does not bother most of us, but it bothered her. Another nun, washing handkerchiefs, splashed the laundry water into her face. It is not necessary to describe more of the well-known vexations of the community life. To bear them for a lifetime demands the exercise of many virtues.

By restraining the impetuosity of emotions and passions, the moral virtues prepare for contemplation. Passions fix the mind on material and sensual things, keeping it from rising to spiritual things. The virtues establish calm in the soul and peace in the religious house.

The virtue of justice also leads to contemplation by giving every person his due, thus removing the causes of strife and discord. A religious appreciates this when he remembers that sins against justice include slander, detraction, tale-bearing, gossip, and other mean manifestations of the human spirit. When most people hear "justice", they absolve themselves from blame because they think of robbery and stealing, but they forget the much wider range of this virtue, especially the area of controlling the tongue. The silence of the cloister prevents many a sin.

Community life prepares for contemplation more directly because it exercises the religious in love for God and love for neighbor. The Order was founded on Charity:

> Before all things, dear brethren, love God and after him your neighbor, because these are the principal commands which have been given to us. These, then, are the things which we command you who live in the monastery to observe: first, that you dwell together in unity in the monastery and have one mind and one heart in the Lord, for this is the reason why you have come together.

The profound wisdom of this passage is brought out graphically by God the Father, who speaks to St. Catherine in her *Dialogue:*

> I require that you should love me with the same love with which I love you. . . . To me in person, you cannot repay the love which I require of you. I have placed you in the midst of your fellows that you may do to them that which you cannot do to me, that is to say, that you may love your neighbor of free grace without expecting any return from him. What you do to him I count as done to me. This my Truth showed forth when he said to Paul, my persecutor,—"Saul, Saul, why persecutest thou me." This he said, judging that Paul persecuted him in his faithful. This love must be sincere, because it is with the same love with which you love me that you must love your neighbor.

Such love is a prerequisite for contemplation, which begins in love, continues in love, and ends in love. Loving God, the soul seeks to find him; when it does so and gazes upon his beauty in contemplation, it becomes more deeply rooted in love and wants to love Him all the more. The contemplative loves all that God loves, especially his fellow men.

Jordan of Saxony, in a letter sent to the friars of Paris, Easter, 1233, stressed this close relationship between loving neighbor and seeing God. Commenting on the failure of "doubting" Thomas to see Christ when the Master appeared to the Apostles on the first Easter day, Jordan wrote:

> Dear brethren, have a constant mutual charity among yourselves, for it cannot be that Jesus will appear to those who have cut themselves off from the community: Thomas, for not being with the others when Jesus came, did not merit to see him. Do you think that you are better than Thomas?

Blessed Jordan has put his finger on the heart of community life. Yet he is but echoing the Scriptures. We read in St. Paul: "Strive for peace with all men and for that holiness without which no man will see God" (Heb. 12:14). St. John the Evangelist is even stronger:

> Let us, therefore, love, because God first loved us. If anyone says, I love God, and hates his brother, he is a liar. For how can he who does not love his brother, whom he sees, love God, whom he does not see. And this commandment we have from him, that he who loves God should love his brother also (I John 4:19-21).

Life in the community also leads the Dominican to contemplation because fraternal charity manifests the Holy Trinity. This truth prompted St. Augustine to say: "Where you see charity, there you see the Trinity." The life of the Holy Trinity is a common life. The Three Divine Persons share the Divine Nature and all the Divine Attributes. They have everything in common except their Personality. Each has his own Personality. This common life of the Holy Trinity is a life of love. The love of the Heavenly Father for the Only-Begotten Son is so great, and the love the Son for the Father is so great, that from their living, subsistent, unique, and mutual love proceeds a Third Person, Substantial Love, the Holy Spirit. The most sublime example of community life is the marvelous interchange of love of the Three Divine Persons. In living the common life, the religious, day by day, witnesses to his belief in the Holy Trinity.

Preparation for the Apostolate

The consecrated life of the Dominican lived in community prepares him to become an apostle, for it engenders in him a love of neighbor founded on solid virtue. In his soul rises love for the brother who stands next to him in choir, who sits next to him at meals, who shares with him the joys and sorrows of the cloister. But love is expansive. It bursts through cloister walls and becomes apostolic; it goes out to the neighbor who lives down the street, who sits beneath his pulpit, who comes to his classroom, who is in far off lands. Willingly the Dominican shoulders the burdens and sacrifices of community life so that through them he might offer prayer and make reparation for souls. When obedience calls on him to go into the pulpit or into the classroom, to surrender temporarily the joys of the cloister and the quiet of the priory, he makes the sacrifice generously, not fearing that these works for others will interrupt his life with God. What he gives to his fellow men, he gives to Jesus. In them he sees Christ.

The profound truth of his neighbor's identity with Christ is brought out in a striking incident in the life of St. Catherine of Siena. Raymond of Capua, who had an intimate knowledge of all the wonders God had worked in the soul of this humble Dominican, shared the episode and described it for us. We repeat it in the dramatic version of Fr. Dominic Rover in his play: *Catherine, My Mother.*

> I remember once in the convent at Montepulciano. She was sick with a great fever and had asked me to come. Even with the fever on her she wanted to talk; so many things had happened to her—new visions, heavenly favors so great she could scarcely find tongue to tell them.

Then the flood of words about God's Blood and
the Bridegroom and the need for a holy hatred of
self, so strong this time that it stung me. It
was, perhaps, the fear and guilt in my soul
or else the devil himself got into my heart, but
I begin to wonder whether it was truly the Spirit
of God who moved her or only the fever, and
whether some mad fever of the soul had not
always possessed her, from the beginning. What
was it—fear, resentment, a trick of the devil?
All those things, no doubt, and all at once. She
lay there in front of me, flushed and babbling
(so I thought) and it struck me that these holy
words were all lies, lies of a wretched woman
possessed of demons or simply mad! Then
I looked again at the virgin and suddenly, it
was not Catherine! It was the face . . . the
face of a man . . . looking up at me, with strong
eyes and a short fair beard. Majestic—like the
Byzantine Christ in the church of Monreale. It
was terror held me there, a great terror, but I had
to speak. "Who art thou? Who?" And the voice
answered: "He Who is." At that very moment
the face vanished and it was Catherine who lay
there, cooled of her fever now, sleeping like a
babe, or caught up in that prayer which for her
was like a long sleep and the end of pain. . . .

The soul in the state of grace is the image of Christ.
The Dominican, by profession a contemplative, is driven
by necessity to love his fellow man. If he has no love for
others, then long hours of prayer, painful hours of study,
meticulous fidelity to the rule will be sterile; they will
never lead him to contemplation. This is the teaching of
St. Paul:

If I should speak with the tongues of men and
of angels, but do not have charity, I have became as sounding brass or a tinkling cymbal.
And if I have prophecy and know all mysteries
and all knowledge, and if I have all faith so as
to remove mountains, yet do not have charity,
I am nothing (I Cor. 13:1-2).

St. Dominic deeply loved his neighbor. As a student at Palencia he sold his personally annotated books to buy food for people suffering from famine. Love for souls kept him up all hours of the night praying and doing penance for them; it awakened his ardent desire to preach and to have the friars preach.

Jordan of Saxony reveals the hidden source of Dominic's love for others:

> His frequent and special prayer to God was of the gift of true charity capable of laboring for and winning the salvation of men, since he deemed that he would be a true member of Christ only when he could devote himself entirely to gaining souls, like the Lord Jesus, the Savior of all, who offered himself completely for our salvation.

Jordan himself was ruled by ardent love for his fellow men. Even as a young deacon at the University of Paris, before he became a Dominican, he burned with love for God and neighbor. It was his custom to rise for midnight matins in a nearby church. One night he met a beggar along the way. Since he had no money with him Jordan took off his belt and gave it to the man. After he reached the church, being early for matins, he went to pray beneath the Crucifix. Kneeling there, he looked up and saw his belt fastened around the waist of Christ—Jordan's reward for his love of neighbor.

To point out these sublime aspects of the common life is not to claim that it is easy to live. There are many obstacles to fraternal charity in the modern environment. To maintain his spirit, the Dominican constantly needs to renew and deepen his motivation, to orientate his life decisively toward love of God and of his fellow men. He can best do this at the foot of the Crucifix. Fra Angelico in his paintings always shows Dominican Saints—Dominic, Peter Martyr, Thomas (the only ones canonized at that date)—absorbed in contemplation of the Crucified Christ. Catherine of Siena perpetually speaks of the Blood of

Christ. It is she who writes in one of her letters: "He who contemplates Christ on the cross with his heart opened by the lance, becomes another Christ, himself loving souls just as he loved them."

Everything about Dominican community life, when it is lived with fidelity and sincerity, enkindles love for God and neighbor. It was designed to do this; Dominic chose the common life as one of the principal means of achieving the ends of the Order: the sanctification of his children, and the salvation of souls through preaching. Community life prepares for contemplation and for the apostolate. The sacrifices accepted and the difficulties overcome in living together form the Dominican religous in the charity which is the very heart of the Order's spirit and apostolate. The charity which rises in the contemplation of the cloister overflows on neighbor in the apostolate. This is the doctrine of St. Augustine: "Before all things dear brethren, love God and after him your neighbor." This precept was repeated by Jordan of Saxony, the successor of St. Dominic: "Always have charity for one another. It is impossible for Jesus to appear to those who separate themselves from the community." Michael Cardinal Browne (then Master General) parapharsed for American Dominicans this precept of the second master general:

> No one, not even our Holy Father, the Pope, can dispense us from love of our conventual life; it is something intrinsic to our state, implanted there by God himself. The touchstone by which we may judge if we, in our apostolate, are following the spirit of our holy Order, will be whether as apostles we retain the love of our holy conventual life.

Chapter VIII

DOMINICAN LIFE

is

SACRIFICIAL

Dominican life is sacrificial, the sacrifice being consummated when the Dominican takes his vows. By the vows of obedience, chastity, and poverty, he consecrates himself as a victim to Almighty God. In the *Book of Leviticus* God laid down in precise detail how each of the sacrifices of the Old Covenant was to be offered. In the Church today, our Holy Mother prescribes exactly how the sacrifice of the Mass is to be celebrated. This determination is in the minutest detail: the number of candles, the color and kind of vestments, and the many actions of the priest—when to make the sign of the cross, when to bow, and when to genuflect. He may not omit or change any of these rubrics.

Our holy Order of Preachers prescribes the laws by which the Dominican must live the religious life in the Rule of St. Augustine, in the Constitutions, in our customs. These regulations are the rubrics by which the

religious sacrifices himself to God. The victim offered is
self, sacrificed by daily living according to the laws of the
Order. This is what the Dominican promised to do when
he knelt before his prior at profession and pronounced
his vows. He promised to obey "according to the Rule of
St. Augustine and the Institutions of the Friars Preachers."
If he lives in any other way he breaks his promise and
violates God's rights over him. Chief among the rubrics of
the Rule and Constitutions are the monastic observances:
silence, fasting, abstinence, wearing the habit, kissing the
scapular, and grace before and after meals, chapter prayers, prostrations and *venias,* the enclosure of the cloister,
and all the customs of community living. The observances
stand among the four chief means—the vows, choral recitation of the Office, the common life with its monastic
observances, and the assiduous study of sacred truth—
chosen by St. Dominic for the achievement of the Order's
ends. Though all of them (except the vows) may be
modified to permit a better adaptation of the Order to
present conditions, the Constitutions state categorically
that they may never be completely eliminated. The observances, immolating the religious as a victim of holocaust,
play a vital part in Dominican life.

The Observances Prepare for Contemplation

The observances are vital to the inner life of the
priory and to the external life of the apostolate. They
were designed by St. Dominic to prepare and dispose his
children for contemplation. By nature they do this as
monastic history testifies. From the days of Pachomius,
the father of monasticism, through Basil, Benedict, Nor-
bert, Dominic, and beyond, contemplative Orders have incorporated these practices into their spiritual life as essential means of living their life. These founders prized
the observances for their many contributions to the community and to individual religious. Among these benefits
was the establishment of an atmosphere of sacrifice. The
observances not only ensure united direction in a community, offering the members fellowship, love and sup-

port, and promoting the apostolate, but also provide opportunity for mortification. Mortification, derived from the late-Latin word *mortificare*, means to kill. The great problem of man since the sin of Adam has been to tame the flesh, flesh meaning our whole fallen nature. The monastic observances help the religious to destroy his vices, leash his emotions and passions, govern his will, die to self. They attack the self-will and pride that lie at the root of all evil. By taming the flesh, the observances prepare the Dominican for contemplation. Whereas the passions entice the soul from the things of the spirit and focus its attention on the things of sense, the observances detach him from material things, and purify the senses, and remove distractions.

The early friars testified to St. Dominic's supreme evaluation of the observances. William of Montferrat, one of his frequent companions, had this to say:

> In all the time we were together, I saw that Brother Dominic kept the rule and observances of the Friars Preachers most strictly. He indeed dispensed the brethren but would not dispense himself. He kept all the fasts prescribed in the rule both in sickness and in health.

Ventura of Verona, who was prior at Bologna when Dominic died there, corroborated William's testimony: "When Brother Dominic was in the priory . . . he conformed to the community in food and drink, kept the rule entirely and fully and did all he could to have the friars keep it." When they failed to do so, he was firm in correcting them. Rudolph of Faenza, procurator at Bologna, went into detail on this point:

> If he saw a brother breaking any rule, he would pass by as though he had not seen it. But afterward, with a mild expression and kind words, he would say: "Brother you must confess your fault!" And with his gentle words he induced all to confess and repent. And though he spoke humble words, he severely punished

their excesses; nevertheless they went away from
him consoled.

Dominic was not content with the mortifications inherent in the faithful fulfillment of the rule. He went
much further in inflicting austerities on himself. His diet
was rigorous, his nightly vigils prolonged. He chastised
himself with hairshirt and discipline. Moreover, Rudolph
tells us: "Brother Dominic always wore an iron chain
girded around his waist next to the flesh. He wore it until his death." Rudolph found the chain when he was preparing Dominic's body for burial. At first he took it as
a keepsake, but later gave it to Jordan of Saxony. John
of Spain spoke of Dominic's vigils and disciplines: "Both
night and day, Brother Dominic was most constant in
prayer. He prayed more than the other brethren who lived
with him and kept longer vigils. He used the discipline on
his body with greater severity and greater frequency than
the others." By such prayer and penance St. Dominic won
the graces of the apostolate.

> God gave him [writes Jordan of Saxony] the
> singular grace of weeping for sinners, the miser-
> able, and the afflicted. He carried their miseries
> in the sanctuary of his compassionate heart and
> poured forth his burning love in floods of tears.

His compassion led him to sacrifices for sinners. The
greater austerities he practiced are not recommended in-
discriminately and should be undertaken only with the
consent of a confessor. But there are a myriad of little
ways of imitating Dominic's mortifications which do not
injure health or impair strength. John of Spain gives some
idea of these: "The Blessed Dominic was frugal in eating
and drinking but particularly as regards any special dish."
Some religious are ingenious in finding mortifications both
unobtrusive and effective. Some religious never lean back
in their chairs. Others are sparing in the use of condiments:
salt, pepper, vinegar, catchup, mustard, and salad dres-
sings. The best mortifications, however, are those that are
inherent in the rule and regular discipline: silence, answer-

ing bells promptly, making inclinations at Office carefully, asking permissions, accepting without complaint restrictions of freedom.

These built-in mortifications should be consciously accepted. Religious should not lose their profit from them by complaining or by doing them through routine without thought of their deeper meaning. The observances should be frequently and consciously offered as acts of love and sacrifice. A religious should not habituate himself to keeping the rules without reflection; keeping them well, perhaps, but never adverting to the fact that they are mortifying, never laying them as homage at the feet of the Crucified Christ.

High on the list of observances are the enclosure, custody of the eyes, and silence. John of Spain tells us how strictly St. Dominic guarded his eyes: "When we walked through the cities and villages together, the witness noticed that Dominic hardly raised his eyes from the ground." The roving eye leads to many distractions and often to sin.

The enclosure of the Second Order is most strict. It prevents both the world from entering the monastery and nuns from leaving it. The cloister of the First and Third Orders, however, is less strict. It is the so-called defensive cloister; it keeps the world out of the religious house but does not forbid the religious from going into the world for the sake of the apostolate. Especially by barring entrance to the spirit of the world, the cloister guarantees to the priory and convent the atmosphere of peace that is so neccessary for prayer and study.

The Dominican is happy when his rule imposes restrictions upon him, when his superiors regulate the use of TV and radio, of telephone and mail box, of visits, trips, and vacations. These restrictions chafe and gall but also protect the religious, giving him the spiritual climate that he came into the Order to seek and reminding him that his true home is the cloister.

Silence is the most important element of monastic discipline. St. James emphasizes it as a test of a true religious spirit: "If anyone thinks himself to be religious not restraining his tongue, but deceiving his own heart, that man's religion is vain" (James 1:26). Elsewhere he elaborates on the control of the tongue; "If anyone does not offend in word, he is a perfect man, able also to lead round by a bridle the whole body." He calls attention to how men control wild horses with bridles, guide great ships with rudders, and tame all birds, beasts, and even serpents, but not the tongue. "The tongue no man can tame . . . it is a restless evil full of deadly poison" (James, 3: 2-10). With this apostolic teaching and the experience of centuries of monastic history to guide them, the Order's Constitutions exhort the brethren to keep silence "with all zeal and diligence." They call it "the most holy law of silence, the guardian of all other observances" and "urge all superiors out of zeal for regular observance to exert themselves to have this most ancient law of silence prevail, notwithstanding any contrary custom whatsoever." The 1955 General Chapter underlined "the most holy law of silence" with these words:

> We admonish the brethren to observe silence even in small houses, especially at table, not only because it is prescribed and is an easy means of mortification for all, but especially because it is altogether necessary for a contemplative life and the study of sacred truth.

What is said of silence can be said of all the observances. All of them in one way or another are a form of silence; they calm the clamor of the senses, still the chattering of imagination and memory, the faculties which feed on the data of the senses. The observances close off these avenues to the soul, barring the distracting thoughts which enter through the highway of the senses.

The friar witnesses during the canonization process of St. Dominic stressed his silence. William of Montferrat says: "The Blessed Dominic always observed silence at the customary times and places according to the regulations. He avoided useless conversation." Forgier of Penna brought out the close connection between silence and preaching: "I never heard an idle or harmful word fall from his lips, or flattery or detraction, but he always spoke of God. And to anyone he met along the road he preached about God and urged the friars to do the same." Ventura of Verona mentioned the solemn silence at night: "When he was traveling he kept silence after compline and made his companions do likewise, just as though he were at home in the priory. In the morning, when he traveled, he had the brethen observe silence every day until about terce." Bonvisus told of yet another kind of silence practiced by St. Dominic: "When the violence of fever took hold of him [during a sickness in Milan], he did not complain about this illness; rather, it seemed he was in prayer and contemplation." Dominic was skilled, therefore, in all kinds of silence: the ordinary silence of the religious house, the solemn silence, the silence which avoids gossip and other sins of the tongue, the silence which refuses to complain.

Monastic Observances and the Apostolate

Monastic observances not only serve their basic function of providing a contemplative climate for the religious life but, for the Dominican, are an essential condition of the apostolate. Religious discipline builds a framework for contemplation, study, and the efficient use of time, factors of utmost importance for apostolic activity. It silences the urging of selfishness and develops a disciplined will, a will that becomes the spring of effective action. The rule eliminates concern for material things, for the needs of daily life such as food and clothing. The religious habit is not only an object of beauty and significance but saves the religious, especially the sisters, the time and trouble of keeping up with the fashions.

The observances also impetrate the graces of the apostolate. Père Cormier, master general from 1904 to 1916, who did so much to revive the Dominican spirit after the damage done by the nineteenth century, brought out a very important point about the discipline of the cloister: "Our whole religious observance," he wrote, "may be considered as a sacramental, endowed by God with a special power of sanctifying our lives whether bodily, intellectually, or spiritually." A sacramental is an action or object instituted by the Church through her approval and blessing as a channel of grace. It becomes the occasion of this grace through the Church's prayer when she blesses the object and though the disposition of the user. The sacramentals are not as effective as the sacraments, which work immediately and directly, but they are precious means of grace. When the Church approves a religious rule, in a sense, she makes all its religious observances channels of grace for religious who follow them. The Dominican Rule and Constitutions bear the stamp of the Church's approval. The discipline they impose will bring Dominicans grace, if they sincerely submit to it. Père Cormier underlined this truth: "All observances, even the least, hide a certain grace and deserve that we diligently carry them out."

The sacramental value of the observances is heightened by the fact that a consecrated person performs them. The person is dedicated to God by profession. The vows give a double value to every action performed under their influence. In the classroom the obedience of the child has one value: the merit of obedience. The obedience of the sister who teaches the child has two values: it is an act of obedience and, though the action of the vow, is also an act of the virtue of religion. The vows can only be lived correctly according to the Rule and Constitutions. This is how the religious promises to obey. When the Dominican keeps his rules, his vows sanctify his actions, in a sense, make them sacramentals. Through them he merits grace. When he breaks the rules or acts contrary to them without dispensation, that action escapes the sanctifying effect of his vows.

The holy habit is the chief sacramental Mother Church has given Dominicans. It is symbolic of the whole religious life, what the religious is, what he aims at, what he hopes to become. These ideals are expressed in the prayer used by the priest to bless the scapular.

O Lord Jesus Christ, who didst vouchsafe to clothe thyself with the garments of our mortality, we beseech thee to bless this garment which our holy fathers have appointed to be worn as a token of innocence and humility, that they who are clothed with it may be worthy to put on thee, Christ our Lord, Amen.

Each time the friar clothes himself with his habit, he reminds himself that his chief duty is to put on the Lord Jesus Christ, that he must do this in a Dominican way, the way of the vows and the observances of the Order. In effect, when he throws the scapular over his head, he hears St. Paul say to him: "Put ye on the Lord Jesus Christ" (Rom. 13:14).

The Dominican puts on Christ by imitating him. A great actor most successfully portrays an historical character when he studies his photographs, his mannerisms, the most minute details of his life, and especially his spirit. An actor who has done this, especially if he has been playing his role for an extended run, tends unconsciously to imitate the character he portrays. If such close imitation can be effected in the case of a fellow man, a religious can more easily do the same with the life of Jesus Christ, a member of the Mystical Body sharing Christ's divine life. The blessing of the scapular speaks specifically of innocence and humility. The colors of the habit exemplify these virtues; its white signifies Christ's innocence; its black indicates Christ's humility: "Learn from me, for I am meek and humble of heart" (Matt. 11:29).

When Dominicans have learned of Christ and put on his virtues then their lives become a convincing argument for their message, a witnessing to the truth that they preach: "We preach a crucified Christ" (I Cor. 1:23).

Keeping the Rules and Constitutions

Since monastic observances have such sanctifying power, the Dominican should keep them well. "All observances, even the least, hold a certain grace in them and deserve that we carry them out diligently." Only when he keeps them will the Dominican get the benefits that St. Dominic wanted him to have from them. It is inevitable, of course, that there will be infractions. Infractions often come from human limitations, sometimes from weakness, sometimes from surprise or inadvertence. One religious, naturally impetuous, blurts out something before he thinks, or breaks the rules because action precedes thought. Another fails through vivaciousness, a third through natural sluggishness. For some people torture begins when the rising bell rings. The heavy sleeper finds it agony to jump up right with the bell. The light sleeper, however, who has no trouble and is always on time, may reap little merit because he has settled into routine and seldom dedicates his promptness to the Lord, or he may make his observance a subject of boastful comparison with his sluggish neighbor: "O God, I thank thee that I am not like the rest of men" (Luke, 18:11).

Since rules and Constitutions do not bind under sin, violations are not sins precisely as violations of the rules. But an infraction may become mortally sinful, if it is done through contempt for the law or through contempt for authority. The actions may be venially sinful, and often are, not because the rules are broken, but because some sinful motive intrudes itself. For example, the religious breaks a rule or fails to keep it through pride, self-love, anger, sloth, gluttony, or uncharitableness. Failing to obey the law through motives of that kind makes infractions venially sinful. If the matter is serious enough, for example, serious defamation of the character of another religious, the infraction may be mortally sinful. The Constitutions of the sisters bring out these truths explicitly:

> The Rule, the Constitutions of the Congregation and the ordinances of the chapter do not oblige

directly under sin. . . . However, the sister can sin indirectly by transgressing the rules and Constitutions if the transgression is committed from some inordinate or culpable motive.

Semi-deliberate faults do little harm, "provided," writes Humbert of Romans, "that you regret your poor observance." When the Dominican is concerned about his violations and does not settle down and live with them, it is a healthy sign, a sign that he is still striving for perfection. But when he no longer thinks a rule is important, then he has stopped working for perfection and is failing in the fundamental obligation that he assumed when he made profession. Christ was most severe with the lukewarm:

> I know thy works; thou art neither cold nor hot. I would that thou wert cold or hot, but because thou art lukewarm, and neither cold nor hot, I am about to vomit thee out of my mouth; because thou sayest, "I am rich and have grown wealthy and have need of nothing," and dost not know that thou art the wretched and miserable and poor and blind and naked one (Apoc. 3:15-17).

In his daily examination of conscience the Dominican should carefully inspect his observance for that day. He should constantly check himself, especially watching the fault which experience has shown to be his special weakness. Since he wears the Dominican habit his salvation is linked with the observance of the Rule of St. Augustine and the Constitutions of the Friars Preachers. Let him break the rules because he despises them, because he no longer cares for perfection, or because he considers observances petty matters that can be habitually disregarded, then the danger flags are up and he would do well to examine his conscience about his own laxity. There is no truth to the legend that a Dominican cannot be lost. He should be constantly concerned about the rule, be sorry when he breaks it, keep it because he prizes it. If this is his prevailing mood, then he is climbing steadily upward, even though he commits unintentional faults.

A page from the *Autobiography* of St. Teresa of Avila illustrates the santifying quality of all Orders approved by the Church and underlines the importance of minute observance of the religious rule. Of all the souls she saw in vision departing this life, only three went directly to heaven. The first was the Franciscan, St. Peter of Alcantara, who escaped purgatory because of his extremely penitential life. The second was the Dominican, Peter Ibañez, one of her confessors. She does not assign a reason for his immediate ascent to heaven, but elsewhere speaks of his high degree of prayer, his penance, and his sanctity. The third was an unknown Carmelite father. Of this last, Teresa writes: "I was amazed that he had not gone to purgatory." But then she remembered that he "had faithfully observed his rule."

St. Therese of Lisieux is a similar case. Her observance of the austere Carmelite Rule with all its rigors and penances was most exact. These were no extraordinary occurrences in her life: no visions, ecstacies, or raptures, as in the case of her great namesake. When Therese lay in her last illness, one of the sisters who was working in the kitchen said to another:

> Sister Therese will not live long and really I sometimes wonder what our Mother Prioress will find to say about her in her obituary when she dies. She will be sorely puzzled, for this little sister, amiable as she is, has certainly never done anything worth speaking about.

People still make this mistake when they talk about Therese; they think that heaven cost her nothing but smiles and roses. But they do not know the Carmelite Rule.

A similar amazement is expressed when people hear that Pope John XXII is said to have remarked when he was canonizing St. Thomas Aquinas: "Prove to me that a Friar Preacher has kept his rule perfectly, and I will canonize him forthwith without any further proof of sanctity." This remark may be legendary, but, if so, it contains a kernel of truth. Sound theology lies behind John's words. It is axiomatic that when the Church stamps a religious Order or Congregation with her approval, its members have a guarantee that its Rule and Constitutions, its way of living the religious life, is a safe spiritual way, a road that leads to sanctity. During seven centuries eighteen canonized saints and at least 285 *beati* have lived "according to the Rule of St. Augustine, and the Constitutions of the Friars Preachers." They belonged to all three branches of the Order, to the First, to the Second, to the Third. Some of the members of the Third Order lived as sisters in community; others as secular tertiaries. Each branch of the Order leads its members to sanctity.

Not one of these saintly Dominicans had heaven handed to him without effort. Every one of them lived the Dominican life under human conditions, conditions never absolutely ideal. There were lukewarm friars during the golden age of the Order, during the days of Raymond, Peter, Albert, and Thomas; even Dominic found timidity and weakness among his earliest disciples. Some of these saintly friars lived in centuries when Dominican life reached the depths, during days of decline and decay. All around them were religious who no longer cared, who were no longer concerned about perfection. The *Dialgue* of St. Catherine of Siena pictures in almost lurid colors the decay that had penetrated the ranks of clergy and religious during the lifetimes of Bl. Raymond of Capua, Bl. John Dominici, Bl. Lawrence of Rippafratta, St. Antoninus, and many of the other *beati.* The experience of these Dominicans of the darker days proves that the priest, sister, or tertiary cannot wait until conditions are just right, until the golden age returns, before beginning to walk the road of holiness. Each Dominican must begin walking at once. He must set out in the spirit of the final words of St. Augustine's Rule:

> May the Lord grant that you observe all these things like lovers of spiritual beauty, breathing

forth the sweet odor of Christ in the holiness of
your life. Not like slaves under the law, but
like those set free by grace. . . . And when you
find yourself doing what is written here, give
thanks to God, the Giver of all good things.
When, however, anyone among you sees that he
has failed in any point, let him repent of the
past, be on guard for the future, praying that his
faults may be forgiven and he be not led into
temptation.

Selected Bibliography

(Abbreviation: VS = La vie spirituelle)

Ancelet-Hustache, J., *La vie mystique d'un monastère de Dominicaines au moyen age d'après la chronique de Töss.* Paris: Perrin, 1928.

Aumann, Jordan, "Dominican Prayer," *The Dominican Bulletin*, VII (1948), 22-30.

Bernadot, V., "La place de la liturgie dans la spiritualité Dominicaine," VS, II (1921), 385-95.

Bézine, S., "La doctrine spirituelle de S. Catherine de Sienne," VS, LXV (1941), 445-48.

"Bibliografia analitica delle publicazioni villa spiritualità dominicana," *Rivista di ascetica e mistica*, VI (1961), 561-88.

Bologni, I., "Contemplata aliis tradere," *Vita Christiana*, VII (1935), 189-204.

Bussiere, Le Vicomte de, *Fleurs Dominicaines ou les mystiques d'Unterlinden à Colmar.* Paris: Poussielgue-Rusand, 1864.

Cachia, E., *The Apostolic Ideal of the Early Friars Preachers.* Malta, 1956.

Cathala, R., "S. Catherine de Sienne, Sa doctrine d'après le Dialogue," VS VIII (1923), 67-92.

—"L'orasion Dominicaine," VS, IV (1921), 396-414.

Clerissac, H., *The Spirit of St. Dominic, a Retreat for Dominicans.* Revised and edited with an introduction by B. Delaney. London: Burns, Oates, and Washbourne, Ltd., 1939.

Colosio, I., *Saggi sull spiritualità Domenicana*, special number of *Rivista di ascetica e mistica*, vol. VI (Florence, 1961).

Colunga, E., "De mysticis dominicanis apud hispanos," *Miscellanea Dominicana*, pp. 190-95. Rome: Ferrari, 1923.

Cordovani, M., "Spiritualità domenicana," *Vita Christiana*, V-VI (1943), 41-60.

Devas, R., "On the History of Mental Prayer in the Order of St. Dominic," *The Irish Ecclesiastical Record*, 5 ser. XVI (1920), 177-93.

La dévotion au Sacré Coeur de Jésus dans l'Ordre de S. Dominique (Anon.). Bar-le-Duc: Imprimere S. Paul, 1929.

St. Dominic: Biographical Documents, ed. F. C. Lehner, Forward by Aniceto Fernandez. Washington, D.C.: The Thomist Press, 1964.

Farren, A.—Ryan, C., *The Dominican Vocation. The Order of Preachers.* Illustrations by Sr. Mary of the Compassion, O.P. New York: Dominican Fathers, n.d.

Ferrua, A., "Miseremini ordinis canonici, saltem vos amici ejus," Memorie Domenicane, LXXIX (1962), 67-70.

"Frères Précheurs," *Dictionnaire de spiritualité.* V (1964), 1422-1524.

Gallais, S., *I tre cardini della vita religiosa domenicana.* Florence: Liberia editrice Fiorentina, 1938.

Gardeil, A., *The Gifts of the Holy Ghost in the Dominican Saints.* Milwaukee: Bruce Pub. Co., 1937.

Garrigou-Lagrange, R., 'La charitè selon S. Catherine de Sienne,"
VS, XLVII (1936), 29-44.
—"'La développement historique de la spiritualité Dominicaine,"
VS, IV (1921), 352-64.
—"La foi selon S. Catherine de Sienne," VS, XLV (1935), 236-49.
—"La espérance selon S. Catherine de Sienne," VS, XLIX (1936),
225-37.
—"S. Thomas d'Aquin. Principes fondamentaux de vie mystique,
VS, VIII (1923), 417-46
—"Unité de la tradition mystique dominicaine sur les rapports
de l'ascetique et de la mystique," VS, Supp. Nov. 1923, 1-27.
Gillet, M.S., *Encyclical Letter on Dominican Spirituality.* Somer-
set, Ohio: Rosary Press, 1945
Greith, C., *Die deutsche Mystik im Prediger-Orden von 1250-1350.*
Freiburg i. B.: Herder, 1861.
Groot, V. de, "S. Dominique mâitre de la vie spirituelle," *Miscel-
lanea Dominicana*, pp. 65-73. Rome: Ferrari, 1923.
Guinassi, E., *Nella vita Domenicana.* 2 ed. Bologna: Studio Domeni-
cano, 1935.
Heath, M.-Starrs, P.M., "The Contemplative Character of Dominican
Life," *Dominica*, XXX (1945), 259-67.
Hughes, Reginald, "Dominican Spirituality" *Review for Religious*,
X (1951), 67-74.
Humbert of Romans, *Opera de vita regulari*, 2 vols., ed. J. J.
Berthier. Rome. Befani, 1888.
Jarrett, B., *The Life of St. Dominic.* Image Books, 1964.
Joret, F. D., "La contemplation mystique d'après S. Thomas," VS,
I (1919-20), 30-43, 91-107, 229-37, 289-95, 383-93.
—*Dominican Life.* London: Sands and Co. Ltd., 1937
Langlais, E. A., *Le père mâitre des novices et des frères étudiants
dans l'ordre de Frères-Prêcheurs.* Rome: Desclée de Brouwer,
1959.
Lajeunie, E., "S. Catherine de Sienne. Sa vie aposotlique," VS,
VIII (1923), 40-66.
Lavaud, L., "S. Thomas d'Aquin. Notes distinctives de sa santité,"
VS, VIII (1923), 341-75.
Lavocat, M. U., 'La spiritualità Domenicana," in *All'ombra dei
____grandi Ordini*, pp. 132-45. Turin: Libreria S. Cuore, 1939.
Lemonnyer, A., "Les prières secrètes dans la vie dominicaine,"
L'anée Dominicaine, LXIII (1927), 269-76.
Lippini, P., *La spiritualità Domenicana*, preface by R. Spiazzi. 2
ed Bologna: Tamari editori, 1958. (An excellent, integrated
theological treatment).
Martin, R., "Le développement historique de la spiritualité Domini-
caine," VS, IV (1921), 352-64.
—*La Vie mystique de S. Catherine de Sienne.* Brusseels, n.d.
Mastroserio, "Il carattere dell'ordine dei Predicatori," *Sapienza*,
(1962), (criticism of Spiazzi, *Vita Dominici*)

Oechslin, R. L., "Spiritualitè Dominicaine," *Vie Dominicaine*, XX (1961), 145-52.

Orlandi, S., "Domenicani, sono monaci o apostoli," *Memorie Domenicane*, LXXIX (1962), 61-66.

Pègues, T., "S. Thomas d'Aquin. Sa *Somme* manuel de spiritualité," VS, VIII (1923), 447-54.

Pepler, C., *The Basis of the Mysticism of St. Thomas* (Aquinas Paper 21, London, 1953).

Petitot, H., "S. Catherine de Sienne. Sa formation spirituelle," VS, VIII (1923), 5-39.

—"S. Dominique. Sa physionomie physique et morale," VS, IV, (1921), 322-51.

Philipon, M. M., "The Dominican Soul, *Dominicana*, XLI (1956), 14-19.

Philippe, P. *The Ends of the Religious Life according to St. Thomas Aquinas*. Athens: Fraternity B. V. Mary, (1963).

—"L'oraison dominicaine au XIII siecle," VS, Supp., Feb. 1948. pp. 424-54.

Portaluppi, A. *Dottrine spirituali. Attraverso la storia della religiosita cristiana*, pp. 67-74, 81-98. Brescia: Morcelliana, 1925.

Pourrat, P., *Christian Spirituality*, II, 196-223, see 224-51, III, 95-105, *passim*, IV, 292-94. Westminster, Md.: The Newman Press, 1953 (first published, 1927).

Raymond of Capua, Bl., *The Life of St. Catherine of Siena*, trans. by George Lamb. New York: P. J. Kenedy and Sons, 1960.

Regamey, P., "Principles of Dominican Spirituality" pp. 76-109, in *Some Schools of Catholic Spirituality*, ed. J. Gautier et al.; trans. by K. Sullivan. New York: Desclée Co., 1959. (Good insights and worthwhile, but disjointed, unduly negative and pessimistic about the possibility of living Dominican spirituality).

Saudrau, A.,*La pieté à travers les âges*, pp. 335-42, 428-31. Angers, 1927.

Sharpe, A. B., "The Ascetical and Mystical Teaching of St. Thomas," *St. Thomas Aquinas* (Catholic Summer School Papers, Cambridge, 1924), ed. C. Lattey, pp. 204-226, Cambridge: W. Heffer and Sons Ltd., 1925.

Shuster, E. J., "Spanish Dominican Spirituality," *Cross and Crown*, IX (1957), 171-81.

Spiazzi, R., "Saint 'Agostino e le origini della scuola Domenicana di spiritualità," *Memorie Domenicane*, LXXIV (1957), 154-82. (historico-theological approach. A tendency to exaggerate the canonical element to the detriment of the monastic).

—*Vita Dominici. Lo spirito e la regola di San Domenico*. Rome: Presbyterium, 1961. (see review by S. Orlandi in *Memorie Domenicane*, LXXIX (1962), 61-66.

Susso, Henry, *The Exemplar. Life and Writings*, 2 Vols., ed. N. Heller; trans. Sr. M. Ann Edward. Dubuque: The Priory Press, 1962.

Théry, G., "Caractères généraux de la spiritualité dominicaine,"
   VS, Supp., Jan. 1938, pp. 22-39.
—"La vie spirituelle d'après les premiers mâitres Dominicains,"
   VS, L (1937), 150-75.
Townsend, A. (trans.) *Dominican Spirituality.* Milwaukee: Bruce
   Publishing Co., 1934.
Turcotte, D. A., *Meditations sur l'ideal Dominicain.* Montreal,
   1942. Italian trans.: *L'ideale Domenicano.* Bologna: Tamari
   editori, 1961.
Vicaire, M. H., "Dominique (Saint)," *Dictionaire de spiritualité,*
   III, 1519-32. Paris: Beauchesne, 1957.
V. Walgrave, "L'avenir des ordres actifs à base monastiques," VS,
   Supp., May, 1963, 219-20.
—*Essai d'autocritique d'un ordre religieux. Les Dominicains en fin
de concile* (Brussels: Editions du cep, 1966).
Walz, A., "S. Catherine de Sienne et le Sacré Coeur," VS LXXVI
   (1947), 891-902.
—'Dominikanische Herz Jesu-Auffassung," in *Cor Jesu. Commen-
   tationes in litteras encyclicas "Haurietis aquas,"* II, 51-95.
   Rome: Herder, 1959.
—*De veneratios divini Cordis Jesu in ordine Pradicatorum.* 2 ed.
   Rome: Angelicum, 1937.
Wilms, H., *Das Beten der Mystikerinnen.* 2 ed. Freiburg i. B.
   Herder, 1923.
—*Das Tugendstreben der Mystikerinnen dargestellt nach alten
   Chroniken der deutschen Dominikannerinnen.* (Vecta in O.:
   Albertus Magnus Verlag, 1927).

Made in the USA
Coppell, TX
27 March 2020